T0126166

Birds of Prey
of the South

FIELD GUIDE

by Stan Tekiela

Adventure Publications
Cambridge, Minnesota

To all people who love the raptors as I do. May this book guide you through a lifetime of enjoying them all the more.

Acknowledgments

I would like to thank the following photographers, falconers, biologists and wonderful friends for their assistance in obtaining many of the amazing images in this book. I wish you all great success in each of your raptor endeavors.

Mark Alt, Grant Anderson, Rick and Nora Bowers, Amber Burnette, Peggy Callahan, Chase Delles, Deanne Endrizzi, Ron Green, Lee Greenly, Karla Kinstler, Andy Kramer, Mike Lentz, Jill Nezworski, Frank and Kate Nicolette, David and Adrienne Olson, Vic Peppe, Candy and Steve Ridlbauer, Pete Riola, Sam Riola, Sharon Stiteler, Frank Taylor, Brian K. Wheeler, Jim Zipp

Special thanks to Brian K. Wheeler, author, raptor expert, wildlife photographer and friend, for reviewing this field guide. Your extensive raptor knowledge is greatly appreciated.

Edited by Sandy Livoti

Cover and book design and nest illustrations by Jonathan Norberg

Quick-compare illustrations and raptor silhouettes by Dudley Edmondson except the following by Julie Martinez: Gray Hawk, Aplomado Falcon, Hook-billed Kite, White-tailed Kite, Short-tailed Hawk, Snail Kite, Harris's Hawk, Common Black-Hawk, White-tailed Hawk, Crested Caracara, Zone-tailed Hawk, Black Vulture, Elf Owl, Ferruginous Pygmy-Owl, Flammulated Owl, Western Screech-Owl

Range maps by Anthony Hertzel

Cover photo: Red-tailed Hawk by Stan Tekiela

See pages 237–238 for photo credits by photographer and page number.

10 9 8 7 6 5 4 3 2

Birds of Prey of the South Field Guide
Copyright © 2013 by Stan Tekiela
Published by Adventure Publications, an imprint of AdventureKEEN
310 Garfield Street South
Cambridge, Minnesota 55008
(800) 678-7006
www.adventurepublications.net
All rights reserved
Printed in China
ISBN 978-1-59193-381-6 (pbk.)

TABLE OF CONTENTS

BIRDS OF PREY OF THE SOUTH

Birds of prey are a diverse group of birds that have captured and held the attention of casual bird watchers and serious birders alike. Also known as raptors, these predatory birds include an amazing array of falcons, kites, hawks, eagles, vultures, owls and the Osprey. All varieties of raptors can be found during the day or throughout the night in nearly all habitats. Falcons are the fastest fliers, while kites are airborne acrobats, chasing insects high in the sky. Hawks, our most common raptor, are seen deep in woods or hunting along forest edges, in open fields and over prairies. Eagles and Ospreys are among the largest and most majestic birds of prey, visible near lakes and rivers. Most raptors are efficient predators, but vultures scavenge for their food without killing anything. Owls, both small and large, are flight masters of the dark.

Despite the wide diversity within the group, raptors physically have much in common. Many are large and powerful, with unsurpassed abilities to catch prey. In fact, the word "raptor" comes from the Latin term *rapere* and means "to seize or grab." Exceptionally strong feet, and toes tipped with dagger-like long nails are perfect for catching and killing small animals. A large curved bill allows raptors to tear flesh and crush bone. Raptors usually have relatively large eyes and better vision than people. Eagles, for example, can see much greater distances, and owls can see better in low-light environments. Most birds of prey have keen hearing—twice that of people. Many predatory birds are also masters of the sky, and people are fascinated by their flight. Propelled up by a single flap, they glide on outstretched wings to dizzying heights, or fly in almost total darkness. These extraordinary physical abilities set raptors apart from all other species of birds. It's no wonder we are thrilled by the sight of these magnificent creatures.

To help you enjoy these birds, *Birds of Prey of the South* has been designed as a handy pocket guide for quickly and easily identifying all 45 raptor species found in the South, including Alabama, Arkansas, Florida, Georgia, Louisiana, Mississippi, North Carolina, Oklahoma, South Carolina, Tennessee, Texas, Virginia and West Virginia—a total of 13 states. Some raptor species included this full-color photographic guide are more common than others. Only a few are considered rare.

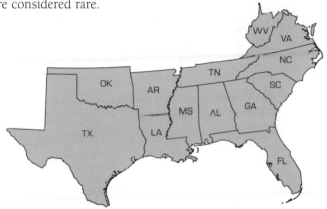

TIPS FOR IDENTIFYING BIRDS OF PREY

Identifying raptors isn't as difficult as it may seem. Follow a few basic strategies, and you'll increase your chances of successfully identifying most birds of prey you see!

One of the first and easiest things to do when you see a new bird of prey is to note its overall shape. You won't always get a good look at a raptor, but noting the shape of its head, wings, tail or body may be all you need to identify it. Silhouettes of each raptor are provided on the description pages to help you confirm your identification. On quick-compare pages, photographs, illustrations and silhouettes will help you to identify a raptor whether it is in flight or perching.

In Flight

Noting the flight habits of an unknown raptor can help you identify it. You may not recognize all flight characteristics or patterns immediately, but with practice you'll greatly increase your ability to identify birds of prey when they are in flight.

Falcons are generally some of the smallest, but fastest, birds of prey. Quick, agile fliers with long tapered wings, they are often seen actively flapping in a direct flight pattern or hovering (turning into wind and quickly flapping), gliding only when absolutely necessary. They are well known for their ability to change direction quickly and achieve incredibly fast speeds when diving onto prey or during courtship. Falcon species in the South include the American Kestrel, Merlin and Crested Caracara, along with Aplomado, Prairie and Peregrine Falcons.

Kites are slim-bodied birds of prey with long falcon-like wings and long tails. They have a unique bouncy flight, frequently described as buoyant. They change directions quickly, flying up and down as they chase after insects in midair. Active fliers, they don't spend much time gliding. Wing beats are often slow and can seem stiff. Five species seen in the South are the Snail, Mississippi, Hook-billed, White-tailed and Swallow-tailed Kites.

Hawks are divided into two groups—buteo and accipiter. Buteos are medium to large hawks with heavy bodies, short tails and relatively long, wide wings. They tend to fly by flapping slowly and heavily for a few strokes, usually in a series of 3–6 beats, then gliding on outstretched wings into a series of tight circles until they gain enough altitude to soar. They are also known to perch in wide-open areas to hunt. Buteos in the South include the Gray, Ferruginous, Red-shouldered, Red-tailed, White-tailed, Zone-tailed, Short-tailed, Rough-legged, Broad-winged, Harris's and Swainson's Hawks, and the Common Black-Hawk.

Accipiters are small to medium woodland hawks with slender bodies, long narrow tails and short, stubby, rounded wings.

Their compact design allows them to maneuver around trees while pursuing small birds. They fly in a very characteristic flap-flap-flap-glide pattern consisting of a short, quick burst of flutter-like wing beats followed by a short glide. In the South, accipiters include Sharp-shinned and Cooper's Hawks, as well as Northern Goshawks.

The harrier is also a hawk, but it is not a buteo or an accipiter. It is the easiest raptor to identify by the flight pattern. Harriers have an extremely low, roller-coaster-like flight that follows every contour of land and vegetation. Wings are slightly raised in a V when gliding, and wing beats are smooth and full. Interspersed in this highly characteristic flight are sudden drops to the ground to pounce on prey. There is just one species of harrier in North America, the Northern Harrier.

Eagles usually fly holding their long, broad, round-tipped wings directly out from their sides. These birds aren't fast fliers, but they flap deeply and powerfully. Eagles often soar with outstretched wings, not flapping for extended distances, rarely teetering from side to side, like vultures. Two types of eagles in the South are the Bald Eagle and Golden Eagle.

Ospreys do less gliding and flap more often than Bald Eagles. They have narrow angled wings unlike the wings of eagles. Their bodies and heads seem to bob up and down with each pump of the wings. These raptors fly with almost stiff wing beats that seem to originate near the wrist, not at the shoulder like the other birds of prey. There is only one species of Osprey.

Vultures fly on long, broad, round-tipped wings, holding them above the level of their bodies in a slight V shape. Their flight pattern consists mainly of gliding interspersed with a few shallow wing beats. During a glide, they frequently teeter back and forth from wing tip to wing tip. Two vulture species that occur in the South are the Black Vulture and Turkey Vulture.

Perching

Identifying a raptor that is perched on a tree branch, power pole or other object may be easier than trying to identify one that is flying. Unlike birds in flight, which often fly out of view quickly, perching birds allow you more time to observe them. In general, birds of prey will usually perch upright on branches or poles. This is unlike crows, ravens and other large birds or even smaller songbirds, which lean out over their feet and approach a more horizontal position. All of this changes, however, in strong winds, when nearly all raptors lean hard into the wind and sit nearly horizontal.

A perched falcon has a flat-topped, compact head, long tail and appears wider in the middle. Falcons often have bold, dark facial marks that appear like a mustache, called a malar, which help identify them while they perch. These birds tend to lean farther out over their feet (more like a songbird) than other birds of prey. Watch for some falcon species to pump their tails up and down directly after landing.

Kites perch upright with their long wings and tail projecting well beyond what you'd expect to see in a perching hawk. The round heads and long necks of kites will be obvious when they perch. Because these birds hunt while in flight, you will be more likely to see them flying to and from perches, chasing flying insects, rather than perched in a tree.

Buteo hawks are easy to identify when perched because of their relatively small heads, large broad bodies and short tails. They are frequently seen out in the open, along roads or in fields and prairies, making them easy to spot.

Smaller accipiters will rarely perch out in the open. Instead, these woodland hawks sit on tree branches for short periods, then fly off to other temporary perches in search of prey. They have smaller heads, narrower bodies, longer tails and less defined shoulders than buteos.

Harriers usually perch on the ground and occasionally on low posts. They have small heads, slender bodies and long narrow tails. Look for unusual owl-like facial disks to help identify this hawk when it is stationary.

Eagles are enormous birds of prey that perch bolt upright, often lowering their bodies over their legs and feet. They tend to look like the trunk of a tree when perching because they are so wide-bodied and dark. Just their size alone should be enough to identify them in a tree.

Ospreys appear eagle-like when perching, but they are smaller than eagles, with smaller heads and less impressive bills. Their long wings project well beyond their tails when perching. To differentiate an Osprey from an adult Bald Eagle, look for its white chest and belly.

Black Vultures and Turkey Vultures aren't often seen perching. When they do perch, they usually hold their wings outstretched to sun themselves, dry out their feathers after a rainstorm or warm up first thing in the morning after a cool night. While this behavior makes them easy to identify when stationary, you are more likely to see these birds flying. Look for their naked heads and dark bodies to help identify.

Owls seen during the day usually will be perching, which often allows you to get a good look. These birds are easy to identify because they sit upright on branches, often with legs hidden in their belly feathers. They also have large round heads with large eyes positioned in front of their heads, thick compact bodies and short tails. Some owls have tufts of feathers on their heads, which appear like horns.

WHAT MAKES A BIRD OF PREY?

All predatory birds share some similar characteristics. Many have relatively large, sharp hooked bills to dispatch prey with a deep bite to the back of the neck at the base of the skull, which severs the spinal cord. Others squeeze prey to death or eat it alive. After a kill, raptors use their beaks to cut and tear flesh and crush bones.

With the exception of vultures, predatory birds have powerful feet, long toes and exceptionally sharp, long nails, called talons. Feet and toes are used to grasp and hold prey. Some birds can actually kill just with the feet. Eagles can do this, some exerting up to 500 pounds (225 kg) of pressure per square inch. Because feet are usually used to capture and hold prey, the importance of a raptor's foot cannot be overstated.

Powerful eyesight is probably the single most important feature of most birds of prey. Nearly all raptors hunt by using their eyes. Any damage to the eyes usually results in the demise of the bird. Eyes of raptors are large in proportion to their heads and fixed in their sockets. Larger eyes increase the vision power but force a raptor to turn its head to look around. Owls, which have eyes positioned in the front of their faces, can see up to 100 times better than people in a low-light situation. Hawks, eagles and other raptors, which have eyes positioned more on the sides of their heads, can see at least 10 times better than people in daylight conditions. All raptors have two sets of eyelids. The outer eyelid is similar to a human eyelid and functions in nearly the same way in most birds. A thin, usually semitranslucent inner eyelid, called the nictitating membrane, cleans and moistens the cornea.

Besides keen eyesight, some raptors have outstanding hearing. Owls are known for hunting by sound. Their ears are hidden under feathers on the face, near the eyes. Great Horned Owls can hear a mouse under as much as a foot of snow. It is said that if an owl can see you, it can probably also hear your heart beat.

Most predatory birds are not brightly colored. Nearly all raptors are light to dark brown, black and white, grayish blue or some combination of earth tones. These colors help them to blend in with their environments.

RAPTOR ANATOMY

Males look identical to females in most raptor species. However, in many species females tend to be slightly or noticeably larger. Throughout the text, the words "slightly" or "noticeably" are used to describe size differences between sexes. When females are only 1–2 inches (2.5–5 cm) larger, "slightly" larger is used. Females at least 3 inches (7.5 cm) larger are referred to as "noticeably" larger. It is thought that egg laying, incubation and protection of eggs or young while still in the nest are reasons for this size discrepancy, or that since the male does most of the hunting, his smaller, more agile size allows him to be a more efficient hunter. Either way, it is not completely clear why in many species females are larger than males.

Juvenile raptors often don't look like their parents for the first couple years. They do not need the adult plumage (such as the white head and tail of the adult Bald Eagle) to impress a mate, so they often have less dramatic plumage. Many predatory birds live long lives and take several years to become mature and sexually active, at which time they obtain adult breeding plumage.

It's easier to identify and talk about raptors when you know the names of their body parts. For instance, it's more effective to use the word "scapular" to describe the region on the back near the shoulder of a Red-tailed Hawk than to try to describe it.

Labeled images on the next two pages point out basic parts of a raptor. Because one image cannot show all the parts necessary, there are several examples of common birds of prey with labels. Every attempt has been made to label all parts of a bird with the terminology used in the text; however, not all terminology shown on the anatomy pages is used elsewhere in this book.

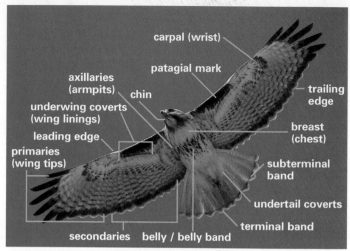

Underside (Ventral)

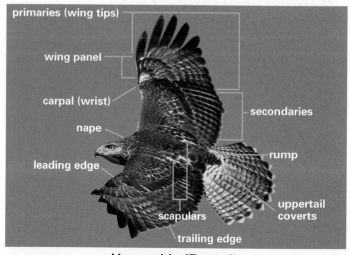

Upperside (Dorsal)

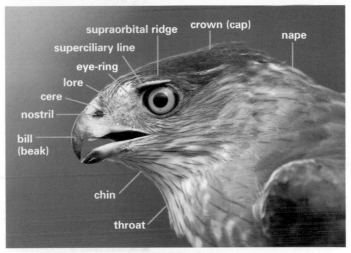

supraorbital ridge
crown (cap)
nape
superciliary line
eye-ring
lore
cere
nostril
bill (beak)
chin
throat

Facial Marking

supraorbital ridge
crown (cap)
eye-ring
lore
cere
nostril
nape
bill (beak)
malar (mustache mark)
breast (chest)

Facial Marking

RAPTOR NESTS

Most birds of prey construct platform nests. Several species build a ground nest. Some falcons scratch a shallow depression into dirt, called a scrape. A few owl species move into natural cavities or old woodpecker holes. Others simply take over existing nests of different bird species such as crows and hawks. The following describes the different types of nests used by raptors of the South.

The **platform nest** is a simple gathering of sticks laid horizontally in a tree fork or on a couple of branches near the tree trunk. This is most common in the hawks. It usually has a shallow depression in the center, which is sparsely lined with dry grass or feathers for cushioning eggs and young. Sticks and branches are collected from the local area. Often they will bring in branches with green leaves still attached. Raptors will occasionally get material for these nests by flying by a dead tree branch, grabbing it and snapping it off. This behavior is common in Ospreys and Bald Eagles.

The size of the sticks used in a platform nest is directly proportional to the size of the bird constructing it. So don't expect to see a small Sharp-shinned Hawk sitting in a huge platform nest. Most of those nests are continually being enlarged and rearranged by large raptors over many years and can be used for two decades or more, depending on the strength of supporting structures. Bald Eagles, for instance, will accumulate so many sticks over the years that some of their nests can be more than 10 feet (3 m) deep and weigh more than 2,000 pounds (900 kg).

Usually both mates construct a nest. In spring (sometimes fall and even winter) mated pairs reestablish their bond by bringing more sticks to their nest. Occasionally a nest grows so large that it either falls under its own weight or is blown down in a storm.

platform nest **ground nest** **scrape** **cavity nest**

A young pair of raptors often doesn't build a nest that is large or strong enough to successfully support a family. While it may take up to several weeks for a young pair to build a typical stick nest, it could take two or more years of work to construct a well-built nest, and several generations of use to get it just right.

Occasionally a pair of young birds will start building a nest but won't lay eggs. The following year they may return to add more sticks to the original structure and then lay eggs. These birds presumably were not mature enough to reproduce the first time they tried. It is not uncommon for a pair of raptors to start constructing a nest, then move to another location and build a second one. This behavior is not clearly understood.

Nests of Northern Harriers are different. This species uses a very simple type of **ground nest**, building it on the ground, or low in shrubs or small trees. Using sticks sparingly, harriers construct their nests with loose grass and other plant material.

A simple nest, called a **scrape**, is a shallow depression scratched into the earth. Used by some falcons, it is usually located on a ledge of a cliff face. It ordinarily will not contain nesting material to cushion eggs or comfort the young. This is the nest of choice for birds such as Peregrine and Prairie Falcons.

Owls don't construct nests. Great Horned Owls, for example, simply take over existing nests of crows, herons and hawks. These owls start nesting early in the year and sometimes are finished raising their young by the time the original owners are ready to move back in. Other owls, such as Eastern Screech-Owls and Barred Owls, use a **cavity nest**, moving into former woodpecker holes or natural cavities to raise their young. They don't bring in any nesting material but simply lay eggs on the cavity floor. Some people have had luck attracting these birds to their properties by installing wooden nest boxes, which mimic natural cavities.

Fledging
The interval of time after a bird hatches until it learns to fly or leaves the nest is known as fledging. Baby raptors are altricial (which means they hatch blind and nearly featherless), and remain in the nest for up to two months. During this time, their eyes mature, flight muscles build and feathers develop. Even after the wings are strong enough to allow young birds of prey to leave the nest, they have much to learn about flight and hunting before they can be self-sufficient.

Unlike many other birds, the young of several species of raptors will return to their nests or scrapes even after they have learned to fly. Using the nest to roost at night, it is also a convenient place for them to rest and get fed. This behavior is seen in young Ospreys. Most other birds don't use their nests again after fledging. Once those birds leave the nest, they never return.

MIGRATION
Most hawks, eagles, kites, falcons and vultures migrate, but some do not. Migration occurs due to a number of complicating factors. One part of this complex puzzle is food. Many raptors migrate to areas with high concentrations of food to ensure that a steady food source, such as insects or small mammals, is available to feed their young.

All migrating raptors are not the same type. **Complete migrators** have predictable movements. They usually leave at set times and go to the same places each year to find available food. Swainson's Hawks are typical complete migrators. At nearly the same time every year, they migrate to the Central and South American tropics. In spring, they return to take advantage of the ample supply of insects, rodents and snakes in the South.

Complete migrators may travel incredible distances, sometimes as much as 15,000 miles (24,150 km) or more in a year, but birds that move only a few hundred miles or just far enough south to escape winter are also complete migrators.

There are other interesting aspects to complete migrators. In the spring, males often migrate a few weeks before females, arriving back at their nesting sites to defend their territories. In many species, females and their young leave early in the fall, usually 2–4 weeks before the adult males.

There are many places to see migrating hawks in the fall. A good place to witness this natural spectacle of migration in the South is at the Corpus Christi Hawk Watch in Texas. Each autumn, tens of thousands of migrating Broad-winged Hawks and other birds of prey pass over this area on their way south.

Raptors that usually wait until food supplies dwindle before they are forced to fly south are **partial migrators**. Unlike complete migrators, which have set migration times and patterns, partial migrators, such as American Kestrels, will move only far enough south or occasionally east and west to find abundant food. In some years, the distance may be only a few hundred miles, while in other years it might be nearly a thousand. American Kestrels and Red-tailed Hawks frequently move into towns and cities where they find enough to eat along busy highways or in backyards. This kind of partial migration, dependent on weather and available food, is sometimes called seasonal movement.

Unlike the predictable ebbing and flowing behavior of complete migrators or seasonal movement of partial migrators, **irruptive migrators** move unpredictably or only every third to fifth year or, in some cases, every tenth year. Irruptive migrations are triggered when times are very tough and food is scarce, or the population density of a species is too high. The Snowy Owl and Northern Goshawk are good examples of irruptive migrators. We can see them in some winters, while in other winters they are absent.

Migrating falcons, kites, hawks, eagles, Ospreys and vultures are daytime (diurnal) fliers that generally rest at night. They hunt early in the morning and begin migrating when soaring conditions are good, after the sun warms up the land. Migrators use a combination of landforms, rivers, and the rising and setting sun to guide them in the right direction. Slowly making their way south or north, they glide on rising columns of warm air (thermals), which hold them aloft. Wind also plays a big part. In autumn, migrators are helped by tailwinds from the north or northwest. These winds push birds along, enabling them to exert less energy than when fighting headwinds. Wind is equally important in the spring, with many birds returning when winds from the south are strong.

Non-migrators do not fly far from their home territory. Great Horned Owls, Western Screech-Owls and other non-migrators are usually sedentary birds that remain in the same area all year long. Ornithologists are now learning that some raptor varieties previously thought to be complete migrators are actually non-migrators. This is the case with Peregrine Falcons. For reasons that are not well understood, some races (subspecies) of this species migrate, while others do not.

HOW TO USE THIS GUIDE

This field guide was designed to be taken with you to help you identify raptors that you see flying or perching. The color photographs and accurate illustrations are ideal for anyone trying to learn more and identify birds of prey of the South.

To help you quickly and easily identify birds of prey, this book is organized by species of birds. Falcons are first, followed by kites, hawks, eagles, the Osprey, vultures and owls. Individual sections are arranged by size beginning with the smaller birds. Sizes are in an average range that includes differences between similar-sized male and female birds, or separate male and female ranges when female birds are much larger than the males.

Special quick-compare pages, beginning on page 24, are useful for studying shapes, postures and colors of raptors. These pages are a great place to start the identification process and make overall comparisons among the birds. For a quick, easy reference, the photographs, illustrations and silhouettes are labeled with common names of the raptors, wingspans or body sizes and page numbers. Simply make comparisons with the bird you see. For detailed information and to confirm its identity, refer to the description pages.

Since many people first see a raptor when it's in flight, the first section of quick-compare pages consists of photographs of the 32 day raptors and 13 night raptors. These show what the birds look like during flight and are in order of wingspan size.

Because birds of prey often show a characteristic shape and noticeable field marks when they fly, the second quick-compare section presents illustrations of the 32 day raptors as they would appear in flight, by wingspan size. Since you are more likely to see perched owls, illustrations show the 13 night raptors as they would appear perching. The owls are organized by body size.

To help identify the 32 day raptors by wing position in flight, the third quick-compare section shows silhouettes of head-on, in-flight views. Categories include wings curved down, wings straight out, wing tips up and wings in a V shape, each arranged by wingspan size.

Photographs of the 32 day raptors and 13 night raptors perched are shown in the fourth set of quick-compare pages, with the species in each group in order of body size.

Since there are only 45 species of predatory birds in this field guide, just paging through the sections is another good way to determine the identity of a bird in question. If you already know the name of the bird, check the index for the page number.

Range Maps

Individual range maps are included for each bird. Colored areas indicate where in the South that a particular predatory bird is most likely to be found. The colors represent the presence of a species during a specific season, not the density or amount of birds in the area. Green is used for summer, blue for winter, red for year-round and yellow for areas where the raptor is seen during migration. Purple is used for raptors that are not very common and indicate the areas where a species has been reported during the previous 25 years. While every effort has been made to depict these ranges accurately, they are only general guidelines. Ranges actually change on an ongoing basis due to a variety of factors. Changes in weather, abundance of species, landscape and vital resources, such as the availability of food and water, can affect local populations, migration and movements, causing birds of prey to be found in areas that are atypical for the species.

Colored areas simply mean bird sightings for that species have been frequent in those areas and less frequent in others. Please use the maps as intended—as general guides only.

Raptors do occasionally move out of their traditional ranges and show up in places where they are not normally found. If you do see a raptor species out of its range, please note the date, time, location and most importantly, try to get a photo to document your finding. Then report your sighting to your local rare bird list service.

Enjoy the Birds of Prey!

Stan

DAY RAPTORS *Ordered by average wingspan*

FALCONS pg. 57 — 1¾' — **Merlin**

FALCONS pg. 53 — 1¾' — **American Kestrel**

HAWKS pg. 97 — 2' — **Sharp-shinned Hawk**

HAWKS pg. 105 — 3' — **Gray Hawk**

FALCONS pg. 61 — 3' — **Aplomado Falcon**

KITES pg. 89 — 3' — **Hook-billed Kite**

FALCONS pg. 69 — 3½' — **Peregrine Falcon**

KITES pg. 85 — 3½' — **Snail Kite**

HAWKS pg. 117 — 3½' — **Red-shouldered Hawk**

Cooper's Hawk

Mississippi Kite

Broad-winged Hawk

White-tailed Kite

Short-tailed Hawk

Prairie Falcon

Northern Goshawk

Northern Harrier

Harris's Hawk

☀ DAY RAPTORS *Ordered by average wingspan*

HAWKS   pg. 145
3¾'

Common Black-Hawk

HAWKS   pg. 125
4'

White-tailed Hawk

FALCONS   pg. 73
4'

Crested Caracara

HAWKS   pg. 137
4¼'

Rough-legged Hawk

HAWKS   pg. 141
4½'

Swainson's Hawk

HAWKS   pg. 157
4¾'

Ferruginous Hawk

EAGLES   pg. 161
7'

Golden Eagle

EAGLES   pg. 165
7'

Bald Eagle

Zone-tailed Hawk

Red-tailed Hawk

Swallow-tailed Kite

Osprey

Black Vulture

Turkey Vulture

🌙 NIGHT RAPTORS (OWLS) *Ordered by average wingspan*

Elf Owl

Ferruginous Pygmy-Owl

Flammulated Owl

Burrowing Owl

Long-eared Owl

Short-eared Owl

Snowy Owl

**Northern
Saw-whet Owl**

**Western
Screech-Owl**

**Eastern
Screech-Owl**

Barn Owl

Barred Owl

Great Horned Owl

DAY RAPTORS *Ordered by average wingspan*

FALCONS pg. 57	FALCONS pg. 53	HAWKS pg. 97
 1¾'	 1¾'	2'
Merlin	**American Kestrel**	**Sharp-shinned Hawk**

HAWKS pg. 105	FALCONS pg. 61	KITES pg. 89
 3'	 3'	 3'
Gray Hawk	**Aplomado Falcon**	**Hook-billed Kite**

FALCONS pg. 69	KITES pg. 85	HAWKS pg. 117
 3½'	 3½'	 3½'
Peregrine Falcon	**Snail Kite**	**Red-shouldered Hawk**

Cooper's Hawk

Mississippi Kite

Broad-winged Hawk

White-tailed Kite

Short-tailed Hawk

Prairie Falcon

Northern Goshawk

Northern Harrier

Harris's Hawk

☀ DAY RAPTORS *Ordered by average wingspan*

HAWKS pg. 145

3¾'

Common Black-Hawk

HAWKS pg. 125

4'

White-tailed Hawk

FALCONS pg. 73

4'

Crested Caracara

HAWKS pg. 137

4¼'

Rough-legged Hawk

HAWKS pg. 141

4½'

Swainson's Hawk

HAWKS pg. 157

4¾'

Ferruginous Hawk

EAGLES pg. 161

7'

Golden Eagle

EAGLES pg. 165

7'

Bald Eagle

HAWKS — pg. 129

4¼'

Zone-tailed Hawk

HAWKS — pg. 153

4¼'

Red-tailed Hawk

KITES — pg. 97

4¼'

Swallow-tailed Kite

OSPREY — pg. 169

5'

Osprey

VULTURES — pg. 173

5'

Black Vulture

VULTURES — pg. 177

5¾'

Turkey Vulture

☾ NIGHT RAPTORS (OWLS) *Ordered by average body size*

| OWLS | pg. 181 | OWLS | pg. 185 | OWLS | pg. 189 |
| 5" | | 6" | | 6" | |

Elf Owl　　**Ferruginous Pygmy-Owl**　　**Flammulated Owl**

| OWLS pg. 205 | OWLS pg. 209 | OWLS pg. 213 |
| 9" | 15" | 16" |

Burrowing Owl　　**Long-eared Owl**　　**Short-eared Owl**

OWLS pg. 229

23"

Snowy Owl

OWLS   pg. 193

7"

**Northern
Saw-whet Owl**

OWLS   pg. 197

9"

**Western
Screech-Owl**

OWLS   pg. 201

9"

**Eastern
Screech-Owl**

OWLS   pg. 217

17"

Barn Owl

OWLS   pg. 221

22"

Barred Owl

OWLS   pg. 225

23"

Great Horned Owl

☀ DAY RAPTORS *Ordered by average wingspan*

WINGS CURVED DOWN

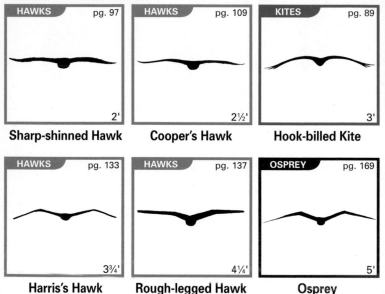

HAWKS pg. 97	HAWKS pg. 109	KITES pg. 89
2'	2½'	3'
Sharp-shinned Hawk	**Cooper's Hawk**	**Hook-billed Kite**

HAWKS pg. 133	HAWKS pg. 137	OSPREY pg. 169
3¾'	4¼'	5'
Harris's Hawk	**Rough-legged Hawk**	**Osprey**

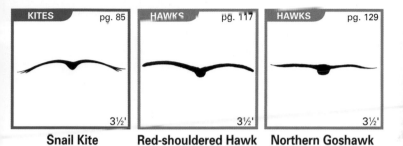

KITES	pg. 85	HAWKS	pg. 117	HAWKS	pg. 129
	3½'		3½'		3½'
Snail Kite		**Red-shouldered Hawk**		**Northern Goshawk**	

☀ DAY RAPTORS *Ordered by average wingspan*

WINGS STRAIGHT OUT

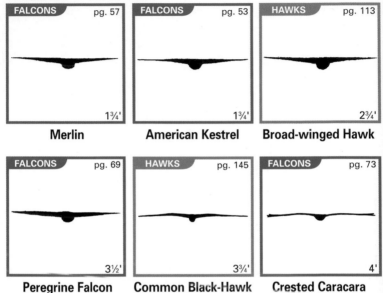

FALCONS pg. 57	FALCONS pg. 53	HAWKS pg. 113
1¾'	1¾'	2¾'
Merlin	**American Kestrel**	**Broad-winged Hawk**

FALCONS pg. 69	HAWKS pg. 145	FALCONS pg. 73
3½'	3¾'	4'
Peregrine Falcon	**Common Black-Hawk**	**Crested Caracara**

WING TIPS UP

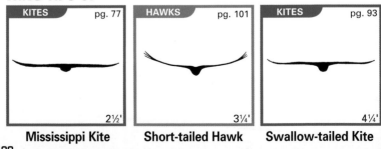

KITES pg. 77	HAWKS pg. 101	KITES pg. 93
2½'	3¼'	4¼'
Mississippi Kite	**Short-tailed Hawk**	**Swallow-tailed Kite**

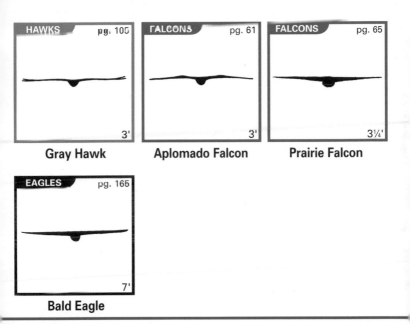

HAWKS pg. 105	FALCONS pg. 61	FALCONS pg. 65
3'	3'	3¼'
Gray Hawk	**Aplomado Falcon**	**Prairie Falcon**

EAGLES pg. 166

7'

Bald Eagle

VULTURES pg. 173

5'

Black Vulture

☀ DAY RAPTORS *Ordered by average wingspan*

WINGS IN A "V"

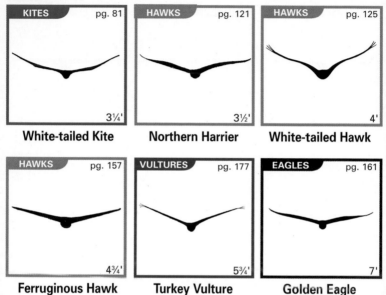

KITES pg. 81	HAWKS pg. 121	HAWKS pg. 125
3¼'	3½'	4'
White-tailed Kite	**Northern Harrier**	**White-tailed Hawk**

HAWKS pg. 157	VULTURES pg. 177	EAGLES pg. 161
4¾'	5¾'	7'
Ferruginous Hawk	**Turkey Vulture**	**Golden Eagle**

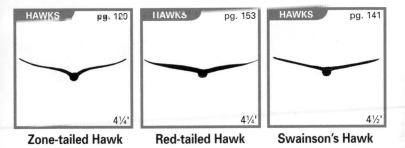

| HAWKS | pg. 120 | HAWKS | pg. 153 | HAWKS | pg. 141 |
| | 4¼' | | 4¼' | | 4½' |

Zone-tailed Hawk   **Red-tailed Hawk**   **Swainson's Hawk**

☀ **DAY RAPTORS** *Ordered by average body size*

FALCONS   pg. 53   10"

American Kestrel

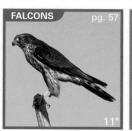

FALCONS   pg. 57   11"

Merlin

HAWKS   pg. 97   11"

Sharp-shinned Hawk

FALCONS   pg. 65   16"

Prairie Falcon

HAWKS   pg. 109   16"

Cooper's Hawk

HAWKS   pg. 101   16"

Short-tailed Hawk

FALCONS   pg. 69   17"

Peregrine Falcon

KITES   pg. 85   17"

Snail Kite

KITES   pg. 89   18"

Hook-billed Kite

Mississippi Kite   **White-tailed Kite**   **Aplomado Falcon**

Gray Hawk   **Broad-winged Hawk**   **Red-shouldered Hawk**

Northern Harrier   **White-tailed Hawk**   **Zone-tailed Hawk**

☀ **DAY RAPTORS** *Ordered by average body size*

Harris's Hawk

Swallow-tailed Kite

Rough-legged Hawk

Crested Caracara

Red-tailed Hawk

Osprey

Golden Eagle

Bald Eagle

Swainson's Hawk **Common Black-Hawk** **Northern Goshawk**

Ferruginous Hawk **Black Vulture** **Turkey Vulture**

🌙 NIGHT RAPTORS (OWLS) *Ordered by average body size*

OWLS   pg. 181   5"

Elf Owl

OWLS   pg. 185   6"

Ferruginous Pygmy-Owl

OWLS   pg. 189   6"

Flammulated Owl

OWLS   pg. 205   9"

Burrowing Owl

OWLS   pg. 209   15"

Long-eared Owl

OWLS   pg. 213   16"

Short-eared Owl

OWLS   pg. 229   23"

Snowy Owl

**Northern
Saw-whet Owl**

**Western
Screech-Owl**

**Eastern
Screech-Owl**

Barn Owl

Barred Owl

Great Horned Owl

Common Name

Scientific name

Family: common family name (scientific family name)

Size: (L) average range of length from head to tail; may include (M) male and (F) female lengths; (WS) average range of wingspan

Weight: average range of weight; may include (M) male and (F) female weights

Male: complete description; some include color morphs or other plumages

Female: physical description compared with the male

Juvenile: full description, often compared with the adults; some include facts about maturation or size

Habitat: environment of the raptor (e.g., forests, prairies, agricultural fields, meadows, mountains, cliffs, backyards, parks, roadsides, bogs, wetlands, lakes, rivers, reservoirs)

Food: what the raptor eats most of the time (e.g., birds, small mammals, reptiles, amphibians, insects, fish, carrion)

Sounds: calls or other vocalizations made by the male or female; may also include juvenile calls or noises created in flight

Compare: Notes about other raptors that look similar and the pages on which they are found. May include extra information to help identify.

Flight: identifying features of the raptor as seen in flight; how the raptor flies; wing beats; types of flight

Migration: complete (regular, seasonal migration patterns), partial (seasonal movement, but destination varies), irruptive (unpredictable movement, depends on the food supply), non-migrator (year-round resident); may include more information

Nesting: kind of nest the raptor constructs and the location; who builds the nest and description of nesting materials; how many broods per year

Eggs/Incubation: number of eggs, color and marking; who does the most incubation and average incubation time; how the incubating parent obtains food

Fledging: average time the young remain in the nest after they hatch and before they leave the nest; who does the most "child-care" and feeding; feeding response of the young

Stan's Notes: Interesting gee-whiz natural history information. This can be something to look or listen for, or something to help positively identify the bird such as remarkable features, unique behaviors and other key characteristics.

male

American Kestrel

Falco sparverius

Family: Falcons (Falconidae)

Size: L 9–11" (23–28 cm); WS 19–24" (48–61 cm)

Weight: 3¾–4½ oz. (108–128 g)

Male: Small bird of prey with a gray head. Two black vertical lines (malar) on a white face and a small rusty brown spot on top of head. Tan-to-white chest with dark spots. Bluish gray wings. Rusty back and tail. Distinctive wide black subterminal tail band and very thin white tip (terminal).

Female: similar to male, slightly larger, with a gray cap, brownish wings, small rusty marks on the chest and belly, many thin dark bands on the tail

Juvenile: similar to adult of the same sex, with more spots on the chest

Habitat: forests, wooded backyards, parks, cliffs, fields, along highways and other roads, rural to urban areas

Food: insects, small mammals and birds, reptiles

Sounds: can be extremely vocal in all seasons; young are the most vocal, especially after fledging; repeats a high-pitched "kee-kee-kee" call

Compare: Male Kestrel is similar to the Merlin (pg. 57), which is not as common and lacks the black vertical mustache marks. Peregrine Falcon (pg. 69) is much larger and has a dark cap and larger mustache marks. No other small bird of prey has a rusty back and tail. Look for the two vertical black stripes on the face of American Kestrel to help identify.

male

male diving

female

male juvenile

female

Flight: pointed swept-back wings; rapid, shallow wing beats alternate with short to long gliding; hovers nears roads before diving to catch prey; flicks tail up and down immediately after landing

Migration: complete to non-migrator, to Mexico and Central America; birds from northern states join resident birds for the winter and move around in search of food, sometimes from rural to urban areas

Nesting: cavity, in a tree, cliff face or wooden nest box; does not build a nest within; 1 brood

Eggs/Incubation. 4–5 white eggs with brown markings; male and female incubate 29–31 days; male does the most hunting and feeds the female during incubation

Fledging: 30–31 days; female and male feed young; male does the majority of hunting and brings food to the female, who feeds the chicks; upon leaving the nest (fledging), the young continue to beg for food and are very vocal, chasing parents around after they capture prey; chicks learn to hunt by watching and copying the behavior of their parents and are hunting by the end of their first summer

Stan's Notes: The American Kestrel is an unusual raptor. Not only do the male and female have different markings (dichromatic), the female is larger than the male (dimorphic).

A falcon, sometimes called K-bird. Was once known as Sparrow Hawk due to its small size. Could be called Grasshopper Hawk because it consumes many grasshoppers. Has the ability to see ultraviolet light. This helps it find mice and other mammals by their urine, which glows bright yellow in ultraviolet light.

Has pointed swept-back wings, seen during flight. Hovers near roads before diving for prey. Perches nearly upright. To help identify this raptor from a distance, watch for it to pump its tail up and down after landing on a perch. While some individuals have been known to become habituated to people, others can be skittish and will fly away when approached.

Adapts quickly to a Wood Duck nest box that is mounted on poles about 7–10 feet (2.1–3 m) aboveground. After the breeding season, kestrels often gather together (gregarious), migrating and wintering in loosely formed groups. Can be antagonistic toward other raptors while in groups, chasing and harassing larger birds until they leave the area.

male Taiga

Merlin

Falco columbarius

MIGRATION
WINTER

Family: Falcons (Falconidae)

Size: L 10–12" (25–30 cm); WS 18–24" (45–61 cm)

Weight: 5½–6½ oz. (156–184 g)

Male: Two varieties in the South. **Taiga** has a steel blue back with a darker head and tail. Rusty wash to the upper chest, sides, wing linings (underwing coverts), undertail coverts and leg feathers. Heavily streaked underwings and breast. Light line above each eye (superciliary). Weak vertical mustache markings (malar). A distinctive wide black subterminal tail band and 1–3 very narrow white tail bands. **Prairie** variety is much lighter, with a light gray back, tan head and lighter marks on breast and belly. No mustache marks.

Female: similar to male, slightly larger, brown head and back, very difficult to tell apart from the male, 1–3 very narrow buffy tail bands

Juvenile: similar to adult female

Habitat: forests, wooded backyards, rural to urban areas

Food: birds, insects, small mammals and reptiles

Sounds: can be very vocal in all seasons; female voice is lower and slower than that of the male; young are the most vocal, especially immediately after fledging, repeating a high-pitched "kee-kee-kee"

Compare: American Kestrel (pg. 53) is overall more rusty and has bold vertical mustache marks (malar). The Peregrine Falcon (pg. 69) has a white face and bold mustache marks. Merlin is the only raptor with multiple narrow tail bands.

Flight: narrow pointed wings and dark underwings; very fast and direct, purposeful flight; powerful, rapid wing beats interspersed with short to long gliding; flicks tail up and down immediately after landing

Migration: complete migrator, to the East Coast, Gulf Coast states, Central and South America; winter resident in the South

Nesting: platform, or cavity on a cliff; takes an old crow or hawk nest and relines it with twigs and some feathers; 1 brood

Eggs/Incubation: 4–7 white eggs with rust brown markings; male and female incubate 28–32 days; male does the most hunting and feeds the female during incubation

Fledging: 30–35 days; female and male feed young; male does the majority of hunting and brings food to the female, who feeds the chicks; upon leaving the nest (fledging), the young still beg for food and are very vocal, chasing parents around after they capture prey; chicks learn to hunt by copying their parents and are hunting by the end of their first summer

Stan's Notes: There are three races of Merlin—Taiga, Prairie and Pacific (not shown). Each appears slightly different from the other in markings and range of color. Only the Taiga and Prairie are found in the South.

Formerly called Pigeon Hawk. Also known as Blue-backed Jack due to the blue color of the adult male's back. Narrow pointed wings, dark underwings and the lack of bold facial markings help to identify this woodland hunter.

Feeds on birds more than insects or small animals. Catches most of its prey in flight, giving a burst of speed close to the ground rather than diving or hovering like the other falcons.

In urban areas, nests in tall conifers and seems to prefer House Finches. Appears to move into urban areas in winter, but it nests in the northern coniferous forests of Canada. Males return to the same breeding territory before the females. The male hunts and provides food for the female during courtship to show he would be a good provider while she incubates. Monogamous, with long-term pair bonding. Nests alone. Defends territory against other birds of prey, including other Merlins. Sometimes young males help other adult males defend territory.

Aplomado Falcon

Falco femoralis

Family: Falcons (Falconidae)

Size: 14–18" (36–45 cm); WS 31–40" (79–102 cm)

Weight: 8–16 oz. (227–454 g)

Male: Large bodied with a boldly patterned black and white head. White chin and breast. Dark belly. Unique chestnut lower belly and undertail. Back dark gray to blue. Long dark tail with many thin white tail bands. Long, narrow pointed wings. Nearly black armpits (axillaries); black speckles extend into wing linings. Dark mustache marks (malar). Dark line through each eye. White eyebrows. Yellow base of bill (cere), legs and feet.

Female: slightly larger than the male

Juvenile: overall lighter than adults, heavy vertical streaks on upper chest, pale chestnut (buffy) color on lower belly and under the tail

Habitat: desert scrublands, open prairies, fields, rural areas

Food: birds, reptiles, small mammals, insects

Sounds: repeats a loud, harsh "kek-kek-kek" alarm call; faster and higher pitched than that of Peregrine Falcon (pg. 69); young are very vocal, especially right after fledging and when begging for food, repeating a high-pitched chittering call

Compare: Peregrine Falcon (pg. 69) has a black hood, shorter tail and lacks white eyebrows. Crested Caracara (pg. 73) has a black back, breast and belly, with much longer legs and an orange patch near the base of bill (cere). Prairie Falcon (pg. 65) lacks bold markings, dark facial markings and a chestnut belly.

adult

adult
dorsal

juvenile

Flight: long pointed wings and long narrow tail; fast and deep wing beats with a rapid direct flight; holds wings straight out when soaring; will hover while searching for prey

Migration: non-migrator; moves around to find food in winter

Nesting: platform, on top of a low tree or yucca; takes an old crow, raven or hawk nest; made with twigs and sticks and lined with grass; 1 brood

Eggs/Incubation: 3–4 white-to-pink eggs with speckled brown markings; male and female incubate 29–31 days; male does the most hunting and feeds the female during incubation

Fledging: 35–42 days; male and female feed young; male does the majority of hunting and brings food to the female, who feeds the chicks; upon leaving the nest (fledging), young still beg for food and are very vocal, following their parents around after they capture prey; chicks learn to hunt by watching their parents and are hunting by the end of their first summer

Stan's Notes: This is an endangered bird that was wiped out (extirpated) from its range in the United States. Once nested in the grasslands of Texas, New Mexico and Arizona. Now being reintroduced in Texas and other places. Reintroduction efforts are slow, but small populations are taking hold in the scrub-lands of southeastern Texas. Populations in Central America and Mexico are stable, and other individuals from Mexico are moving into Arizona. Regardless, it is unlikely to see this bird except in the areas where it was introduced.

Unlike most other falcon species, both sexes appear the same (non-dimorphic), except that females are slightly larger than the males. Often seen flying low and directly across scrublands and grasslands before landing on top of a perch. Will sit and watch for a while, then fly to another perch.

Often hunts small birds and insects on the wing, snatching prey from the air. Will also hunt while perching on vegetation, such as yucca, and power poles. Has been known to work the edges of grass fires, waiting for insects and small animals to flee into the open before snatching them up.

WINTER

Prairie Falcon

Falco mexicanus

Family: Falcons (Falconidae)

Size: M 15–16" (38–40 cm); WS 3–3¼' (.9–1 m)
F 16–18" (40–45 cm); WS 3½–3¾' (1.1–1.14 m)

Weight: M 1–1¼ lb. (.5–.6 kg); F 1¼–1½ lb. (.6–.7 kg)

Male: Thin body with a pale brown head, back and tail. White breast and underwings, completely covered with small brown spots. Black armpits (axillaries), with black speckling extending into wing linings (underwing coverts). Large squared head with a white area behind the eyes. Dark narrow mustache markings (malar). Yellow base of bill (cere), eye-rings, legs and feet.

Female: noticeably larger than the male, with a heavier, nearly black patch on underwing coverts

Juvenile: overall darker than adults, heavy vertical streaks on breast and belly, nearly black axillaries

Habitat: open prairies, fields, meadows, cliffs, parks, along highways and other roadways, rural areas

Food: birds, insects, small mammals and reptiles

Sounds: repeats a loud, harsh "kree-kree-kree" alarm call much like that of Peregrine Falcon (pg. 69); also gives a high-pitched scream; young are very vocal, especially right after fledging, repeating a high-pitched "kee-kee-kee" call

Compare: Peregrine Falcon (pg. 69) is slightly larger, overall darker, with a black hood, wider mustache marks and lacking the dark axillaries and wing linings. Merlin (pg. 57) is smaller, has a blue gray back and lacks dark axillaries and wing linings.

male

adult
dorsal

juvenile

female

Flight: long semi-pointed wings; fast and powerful wing beats with a rapid flight, often soaring and riding thermals; soars holding wings flat; will hover while searching for prey

Migration: partial to non-migrator, scattering widely across most of the western half of the country; seen only during winter months when some individuals move around to find food

Nesting: ground (scrape), on a cliff face ledge or bluff face that overlooks open habitat; nest is a shallow depression scraped in the dirt, not lined with nesting material; 1 brood

Eggs/Incubation: 4–5 white eggs with brown markings; male and female incubate 29–31 days; male does the most hunting and feeds the female during incubation

Fledging: 35–42 days; male and female feed young; male does the majority of hunting and brings food to the female, who feeds the chicks; upon leaving the nest (fledging), young still beg for food and are very vocal, following their parents around after they capture prey; chicks learn to hunt by watching their parents and are hunting by the end of their first summer

Stan's Notes: This is a falcon of open prairies in western states, often wandering and showing up in unusual places during migration and winter. Once it establishes a place to stay for the winter, it typically remains for the entire season, returning to its normal range in late winter and early spring.

The eyes of this bird in proportion to its head are larger than those of any other falcon. During courtship the male performs a strutting display for the female on the edge of the nest along with spectacular aerial displays, all while calling to her. He also brings food to her to prove he is a good provider. Monogamous, and nests alone. Nests may be within a quarter mile of each other if suitable nesting habitat is in short supply. When disturbed at the nest, the male hangs back while the larger, more aggressive female vocalizes and swoops at the intruder.

Perches on telephone poles, cliffs or hovers in search of prey. Jumps from a perch in a burst of rapid flight to overtake birds flying low to the ground. When soaring it will dive from high up, knocking small birds out of the sky to the ground in the same manner as Peregrine Falcons (pg. 69).

Peregrine Falcon

Falco peregrinus

YEAR-ROUND
MIGRATION
SUMMER
WINTER

Family: Falcons (Falconidae)

Size: M 14–16" (36–40 cm); WS 3–3¼' (.9–1 m)
F 16–20" (40–50 cm); WS 3¼–3¾' (1–1.14 m)

Weight: M 1–1¼ lb. (.5–.6 kg); F 1¼–1½ lb. (.6–.7 kg)

Male: A wide-bodied raptor. Dark, nearly black head marking resembling a hood. Steel blue back and tail. Pale white-to-tan breast and underwings. Small black horizontal bars on belly, legs, underwings and undertail. Black mustache markings (malar). Yellow base of bill (cere), eye-rings, legs and feet. Some individuals have a wash of salmon on the breast.

Female: similar to male, noticeably larger

Juvenile: mostly brown with heavy vertical streaks on the breast and belly, overall darker than adults

Habitat: along rivers, lakes, forests, cliffs, bluffs, city parks, along highways and other roadways, rural to urban areas

Food: birds (Rock Pigeons in many cities, shorebirds and waterfowl in rural areas)

Sounds: usually repeats a loud, harsh alarm call near the nest; young give a similar call to beg for food

Compare: Prairie Falcon (pg. 65) is slightly smaller and lacks the nearly black head (hood) and mustache markings (malar). American Kestrel (pg. 53) is much smaller, brightly colored and lacks a blackish hood. Peregrine Falcon is usually identified by its dark head marking, mustache marks and clear upper chest.

adult

adult dorsal

juvenile

juvenile

Flight: long pointed wings; deep, smooth, powerful wing beats interspersed with short gliding; soars with wings flat, often riding thermals

Migration: complete to non-migrator, to southern states, Mexico, Central and South America; non-migrators remain in some areas all year

Nesting: ground (scrape), on a cliff edge; nest is just a shallow depression scraped in the dirt; will also use an artificial (man-made) wooden platform with a dirt and rock bottom, installed on a tall building; not lined with nesting material; 1 brood

Eggs/Incubation: 3–4 white eggs, occasionally with brown markings; female and male incubate 29–32 days; male does the most hunting and feeds the female during incubation

Fledging: 35–42 days; female feeds the young; male does the majority of hunting and brings food to the female, who feeds the chicks; upon leaving the nest (fledging), the young still beg for food and are very vocal; chicks learn to hunt by watching and copying the behavior of their parents and are hunting by the end of their first summer

Stan's Notes: A hunter of many species of birds, especially pigeons and waterfowl. All birds scatter at the approach of a Peregrine Falcon.

Became locally extinct in many regions (extirpated) due to DDT poisoning during the 1930–60s. Was reintroduced by a captive breeding program and released into cities starting in the 1980s. It has since made a great comeback and is doing well. In some areas it may even be more common than it was historically.

Females are noticeably larger than the males. When they hunt together, the female will take the lead and capture larger prey. Hunts by diving (stooping) on pigeons at speeds up to 175 mph (282 km/h) or more, knocking the prey from sky to ground.

Prefers nesting on ledges for a good view of its territory, which is why it has taken so well to high buildings, bridges and tall smokestacks. To provide more nesting habitat, platforms with rocks and gravel have been installed near building ledges.

Monogamous and a solitary nester. During courtship, performs aerial displays and male brings food to the female.

YEAR-ROUND

Crested Caracara

Caracara cheriway

Family: Falcons (Falconidae)

Size: 21–24" (53–61 cm); WS 3½–4¼' (1.1–1.3 m)

Weight: 1¾–2¼ lb. (.8–1 kg)

Male: Unique shape, with a nearly black body and a white breast with fine horizontal speckling. White chin, with white extending up onto the cheeks. Obvious black cap, looking like a large shaggy toupee. Large orange facial skin just behind a large gray bill. Long neck. Long, broad black wings and white wing tips. White tail with a black terminal band, seen in flight. Long, strong yellow legs.

Female: same as male, slightly larger

Juvenile: similar to adults, but brown areas instead of black, and tan areas instead of white

Habitat: open savanna, scrublands, near ranches, rural areas, along highways and other roadways

Food: carrion, mice and other small animals, insects, reptiles

Sounds: often silent; low croaking and guttural sounds, but during breeding season it repeats a loud "wick-wick" sound, often throwing its head over its back while giving the last call note

Compare: Osprey (pg. 169) lacks the black belly and orange facial skin. Aplomado Falcon (pg. 61) has narrow pointed wings and dark facial marks. Black Vulture (pg. 173) lacks white on the head and tail. Look for a bold black and white pattern and long yellow legs to help identify the Caracara.

73

adult

adult dorsal

juvenile

Flight: wide broad wings; glides with wings flat; shallow, rapid wing beats interspersed with short or long gliding; patrols at low elevations along roads at sunrise and sunset

Migration: non-migrator; moves around to find food

Nesting: large platform, in a tree; female builds; 1 brood

Eggs/Incubation: 2–3 white or pinkish eggs with brown markings; female and male incubate 26–30 days; male does the most hunting and feeds the female during incubation

Fledging: 40–60 days; female and male feed young; male does the most hunting and brings food to the female, who feeds the chicks; upon fledging, the young still beg for food and are very vocal, chasing parents after they catch prey; chicks copy their parents and are hunting by the end of their first summer

Stan's Notes: The largest member of the falcon family. Has facial skin that can change color quickly, usually to pale gray and back to orange, when the bird is agitated or excited.

Very different from all falcons and other raptors in North America, using its long legs to stalk and chase prey such as mice. Feeds mainly on roadkill, often coursing along roadways at low elevations at dawn, looking for fresh kills. Will circle, land and walk up to a carcass. Often pulls carrion off the road to eat in safety.

Often in pairs. Sometimes seen with vultures. Vultures may follow caracaras to find food. Caracaras glide on flat wings, while vultures hold their wings up in a semi-V during flight. The white wing tips and white on the head and base of tail are obvious in flight and help to identify the bird as it flies.

Builds a large nest in a tree. Often returns to the same nest each breeding season. Long-term mates but solitary nesters. Pairs defend a large territory. Roosts in trees at night.

Seen in Texas, Florida and Arizona. The Florida population is much lower in number than the others, but it is relatively stable. In agricultural areas it can be a good neighbor, cleaning up dead critters while leaving farm animals unharmed. It is the national bird of Mexico.

Mississippi Kite

Ictinia mississippiensis

MIGRATION
SUMMER

Family: Hawks, Eagles and Kites (Accipitridae)

Size: L 12–15" (30–38 cm); WS 29–33" (74–84 cm)

Weight: 9–11 oz. (255–312 g)

Male: Overall gray bird with a paler, nearly white head and nearly black tail and tips of wings. Dark eye patch surrounding red eyes. Yellow legs and feet. Short, hooked gray bill. Wings have white secondaries, seen in flight from above, and rusty primaries, seen from above and below.

Female: same as male, slightly larger, head not as white

Juvenile: brown breast with white horizontal streaks, alternate dark and light bands on the tail, rusty wing linings (underwing coverts) seen in flight, dark wing tips (primaries) and secondaries

Habitat: fields with scattered tall trees, backyards, parks, near rivers or streams, suburban to urban areas

Food: butterflies, cicadas, other large insects, lizards, small snakes

Sounds: very high-pitched, weak whistle call, descending in pitch when trespassers get near the nest; can be very vocal during breeding season

Compare: White-tailed Kite (pg. 81) is nearly all white with black shoulder marks. Swallow-tailed Kite (pg. 93) has a deeply forked tail and white head and chest. Snail Kite (pg. 85) occurs only in the southern half of Florida and has a much larger hooked bill. Mississippi Kite's gray appearance with the light-colored head and long pointed wings makes it easy to identify. Look for the dark tail and light head to help identify it in flight.

Flight: long pointed wings; wide variety of flight patterns since it hunts for insects in midair; glides with wings fully outstretched and flat when eating in flight; buoyant flight, soaring with wings flat; wings often swept back when diving

Migration: complete migrator, to South America

Nesting: platform, often in a deciduous tree, near the top; female and male build a small, shallow, flimsy nest; 1 brood

Eggs/Incubation: 1–2 white eggs; female and male incubate 29–32 days; each parent hunts for its own food

Fledging: 32–34 days; female and male feed the young still in the nest; male does the majority of the hunting and feeding of young after they fledge; young sit on a branch and give a high-pitched whistle to beg for food; parents bring food and pass it quickly to the young before taking off to hunt again; chicks learn to hunt by watching and copying the behavior of parents and are hunting by the end of their first summer

Stan's Notes: The most common of kites. Common across the South along rivers and open areas that have several tall trees. Often found in small groups feeding together. Has been expanding its range northward up into the Midwest.

Feeds mostly on large insects, taking advantage of large hatches of cicadas and butterflies. Several kites can be seen following livestock, feeding on insects kicked up by the animals. Hunts by soaring or hovering, catching prey in flight or diving down to snatch an insect from tree branches and leaves. Can dive very fast, pulling up suddenly to land softly and smoothly on a branch.

Requires open areas with scattered tall trees for nesting. Will sometimes nest in small colonies of up to 20 pairs, with nests evenly spaced among trees. Leisurely paced mating and nesting; some wait to nest until late summer. Mated pairs aggressively defend nest sites. Often doesn't nest until 2 years of age.

Courting males bring food to females. Non-breeding birds (sub-adults) often form groups within colonies. Sometimes they help construct nests and feed the new young.

YEAR-ROUND

White-tailed Kite

Elanus leucurus

Family: Hawks, Eagles and Kites (Accipitridae)

Size: L 14–16" (36–40 cm); WS 3–3½' (.9–1.1 m)

Weight: 10–13 oz. (284–369 g)

Male: White tail, head, chest, belly and a gray back. Long, pointed gray wings with a large black patch at the shoulders. White underwing coverts with a small black spot at each wrist (carpal) and dark wing tips, seen during flight. Deep red eyes, each with a black eye-ring. In flight, tail is long and narrow, sometimes fanned out broadly.

Female: same as male

Juvenile: similar to adults, with a buffy brown wash to the head and chest, mottled gray back

Habitat: open savanna, wetlands, foothills, washes, near streams, parks, agricultural areas

Food: small mammals (especially voles), large insects, reptiles, amphibians

Sounds: low, weak, brief whistle call; young give a longer whistle to beg for food

Compare: Similar size as the Mississippi Kite (pg. 77), which is mainly gray and has a black tail. The male Northern Harrier (pg. 121) is larger and shares the white wings with dark wing tips, but it lacks the pointed wings and black shoulder patches of the White-tailed Kite.

adult

adult dorsal

juvenile

Flight: long, narrow pointed wings; slow graceful flight with slow deep wing beats; glides with wings fully outstretched and held slightly above the body in a wide V; wings are often swept back when diving; hovers and soars on thermals extensively

Migration: non-migrator; moves around to find food in winter

Nesting: platform, at the top of a tree, well camouflaged from below and open to the top; female and male build the nest with sticks and twigs and line it with grass, moss, rootlets and other fine plant material; 1 brood

Eggs/Incubation: 3–6 white eggs with dark markings; female incubates 28–30 days; male hunts and feeds the female

Fledging: 36–41 days; female and male feed the young still in the nest; male does the majority of the hunting after the young fledge; young sit on a branch and beg for food; parents bring food and quickly pass it to the young before taking off to hunt again; chicks watch and copy the hunting behavior of their parents and are hunting by the end of their first summer

Stan's Notes: Also called White Hawk for its overall color, but the White-tailed is not a hawk. Kites specialize in hunting from the air. Hovers, scanning the ground for rodents. Swoops down to snatch prey. Also eats during flight, reaching down to grab prey that it holds securely with its feet. In flight, shape is falcon-like and plumage color is gull-like.

Breeds in loose colonies, with several nests in a couple acres. Monogamous, often returning to the same nest for many years. Range has increased over the last 50 years due to more farming and more rodents. Much of this range expansion is irruptive. Takes up residency in new areas with high populations of voles until the prey base weakens, then moves away.

At times other than the breeding season, often gathers in large groups of as many as 100 individuals for communal roosting and hunting. The farther north in the range, the less common this practice.

male

YEAR-ROUND
SUMMER

Snail Kite

Rostrhamus sociabilis

KITES

Family: Hawks, Eagles and Kites (Accipitridae)

Size: M 16–18" (40–45 cm); WS 3½–3¾' (1.1–1.14 m)
F 17–19" (43–48 cm); WS 3½–3¾' (1.1–1.14 m)

Weight: 13–16 oz. (369–454 g)

Male: Overall dark gray bird with black wing tips and white rump and undertail. Short black tail with a thin white terminal tail band. Dark red eyes and dark orange legs and feet. A long, sharply hooked, thin black bill with an orange base.

Female: slightly larger than male, overall dark brown, can be uniform in color or covered with small white patches, especially at base of tail and wing tips, white face and chin, bold yellow cere, light orange legs and feet, long hooked bill

Juvenile: similar to female, white breast with vertical brown streaks, more white on body, wings and head, dark wing tips, yellow legs and feet, bill is dark and shorter and less hooked than adult bill

Habitat: wetlands, lakes and other bodies of water that contain snails

Food: apple snails, turtles

Sounds: usually silent; harsh, grating call when upset; juveniles give a similar scream, but coarser

Compare: White-tailed Kite (pg. 81) is nearly all white with black shoulder marks. Swallow-tailed Kite (pg. 93) has a deeply forked tail and white head and chest. Mississippi Kite (pg. 77) lacks a black and orange bill and orange legs and feet. Snail Kite is a habitat specialist and is not seen away from bodies of water.

male

male dorsal

male female

female

juvenile

juvenile

Flight: long rounded wings; slow and floating flight pattern; glides with wings fully outstretched and legs hanging down; buoyant flight, soaring with wings bowed and wing tips down

Migration: non-migrator, moving south in Florida to find food during winter

Nesting: platform, in any vegetation emerging from the water; male builds a small flimsy nest above the water's surface to up to 15 feet (4.6 m) high, sometimes before obtaining a mate, and female helps modify later; nests in nearly any month; 1 brood

Eggs/Incubation: 2–4 white eggs with brown markings; male and female incubate 26–30 days; each hunts for its own food

Fledging: 23–28 days; female and male feed the nestlings; male does the most hunting and feeding of young after they fledge; young perch on a branch and wait for their parents to bring food; parents pass food quickly to their young before taking off to hunt again; chicks learn to hunt by watching and copying the parents and are hunting by the end of their first summer

Stan's Notes: Once known as the Everglade Kite. Not very common, with populations restricted to wet habitats that have ample snails. Feeds mostly on the large apple snail. Will take advantage of times of high water levels, when more snails are available. Quickly and easily extricates the entire snail from the shell before swallowing it whole. Litter piles of empty snail shells accumulate below a favorite feeding perch. Also feeds on turtles. Uses its long curved bill to reach inside the turtle shell and extract meat a little bit at a time.

A highly managed bird in Florida and considered endangered. The state population was reduced to fewer than 24 individuals by the 1960s due to wetland draining and shooting. Because of the specialized habitat and food requirements, this species is not adapting well to the changing environments in Florida, and populations are still decreased.

Nests in loose colonies consisting of a few pairs. Occasionally nests so low in grasses that the nests are run over and destroyed by airboats. Nesting success increases with higher water levels. Unusual because it can reproduce anytime over a 10-month period each year. Can start breeding at 10–12 months of age.

male

Hook-billed Kite

Chondrohierax uncinatus

Family: Hawks, Eagles and Kites (Accipitridae)

Size: L 17–20" (43–50 cm); WS 34–37" (86–94 cm)

Weight: 8–12 oz. (227–340 g)

Male: Overall light gray with a lighter gray breast and belly. Gray and off-white wing tips. Light blue-to-white eyes. Greenish patch of skin (cere) with a spot of bold yellow above. Yellow legs and feet. A very large, thick, hooked bill with a black tip. Long tail with gray and black bands.

Female: slightly larger than male, overall dark brown with gray cheeks and chin, a rufous neck, breast and belly with large horizontal white barring on the breast and belly

Juvenile: similar to female, with white cheeks and white extending onto the neck, a white chest with thin brown horizontal streaks, less bold cere

Habitat: scrublands, thorn scrub, brushy wetlands, lowland forests, along rivers and lakes

Food: tree snails

Sounds: rapid rattling call that sounds more like a woodpecker or songbird

Compare: Similar size as Snail Kite (pg. 85), which lives in Florida; Hook-billed is found only in Texas. Smaller than the White-tailed Kite (pg. 81), which has a white head and chest and a tiny bill. Larger than the Mississippi Kite (pg. 77), which lacks the large hooked bill. Hook-billed Kite is very uncommon and is only occasionally seen in extreme southern Texas.

male

female

juvenile

juvenile

female

Flight: long broad wings with very rounded tips; slow and deep flaps; glides with wings slightly down; buoyant flight, soaring with wings down and wing tips slightly up; doesn't often soar up high since its food source is in thick scrub

Migration: non-migrator; moves around in winter to find food

Nesting: platform, in a thick tangle of branches in any wood vegetation; male and female build a small, shallow, flimsy nest of sticks and branches no higher than 15 feet (4.6 m); 1 brood

Eggs/Incubation: 2–3 white eggs with brown markings; male and female incubate, number of days is not known; each parent hunts for its own food

Fledging: unknown days; female and male feed young independently at the nest; male does the most hunting and feeding of nestlings; young sit on a branch and wait for food; parents bring food and pass it to the young quickly before taking off to hunt again; chicks learn to hunt by watching and copying the parents and are hunting by the end of their first summer

Stan's Notes: A very uncommon species found only in the extreme southern tip of Texas. Main population occurs across Mexico and into central America. Requires specialized habitat of thick scrub that supports a large population of tree snails.

Feeds nearly exclusively on tree snails, which are much smaller than the more familiar apple snail in Florida. Moves around, collecting snails attached to trees. Feeds at a favorite spot near the nest. Uses its small feet to clutch a snail, much like a parrot, while feeding. Unlike Snail Kite (pg. 85), which cleanly extracts snails from shells, Hook-billed Kite crunches shells and works to extract its prey. Huge piles of shells sometimes pile up under perches. It is thought that the bill size of local populations may be in direct association with the snail size in the region.

Very little study has been done on this species. It is unlike any other raptor, with a glassy, light blue-to-white eye color that gives a distinctive expression. Between the eyes and the bill is a greenish patch of skin (cere) topped by a spot of bold yellow. It has unusually short legs for unknown reasons, and it gives a repetitive call that sounds more like a woodpecker or songbird rather than a raptor.

SUMMER

Swallow-tailed Kite

Elanoides forficatus

Family: Hawks, Eagles and Kites (Accipitridae)

Size: L 18–23" (45–58 cm); WS 4–4½' (1.2–1.3 m)

Weight: 14–16 oz. (397–454 g)

Male: White head, breast and belly. Black back, wings and tail. Long, narrow pointed wings. White underwing coverts and black trailing edge, seen during flight. Long, deeply forked tail. Back and wings change color with light conditions, appearing metallic greenish blue.

Female: same as male

Juvenile: similar to adults, with a shorter tail and buffy brown wash to the head and chest that lasts only a few weeks

Habitat: open woods, near river bottoms, fields with scattered tall trees, backyards, parks, near streams, suburban to urban areas

Food: large insects such as bees, butterflies, dragonflies, beetles and cicadas; also eats lizards, small snakes, frogs, small mammals

Sounds: very high-pitched, weak whistle call, descending in pitch when intruders are near the nest; can be very vocal during breeding season

Compare: Osprey (pg. 169) is similar in size and shares the black and white pattern, but lacks a long forked tail. Mississippi Kite (pg. 77) is much smaller than Swallow-tailed and is gray with a black tail that does not fork. No other bird of prey in the South has a forked tail as deep as the Swallow-tailed Kite.

juvenile

adult

juvenile

Flight: long, narrow pointed wings and forked tail; many flight patterns because it hunts insects in midair; glides with wings fully outstretched and flat when eating in flight; buoyant, agile flight, soaring with wings flat and the forked tail opening and closing like scissors; wings often swept back when diving; rarely hovers, but soars on thermals extensively; gathers in flocks for winter migration

Migration: complete migrator, to the tropics of Central and South America

Nesting: platform, often in a deciduous tree, near the top; female and male build a small, shallow, flimsy nest; 1 brood

Eggs/Incubation: 2–4 white eggs with dark markings; female and male incubate 26–28 days; each parent hunts for its own food; both parents feed the young

Fledging: 36–42 days; female and male feed the young still in the nest; male does the majority of the hunting and feeding of young after they fledge; young sit on a branch and give a high-pitched whistle to beg for food; parents bring food and pass it quickly to the young before taking off to hunt again; chicks learn to hunt by watching and copying the behavior of parents and are hunting by the end of their first summer

Stan's Notes: This species is seen mostly in Florida, Georgia and South Carolina. Also found in Alabama, Mississippi and Louisiana, crossing into Texas. Nested in the Northeast and Midwest during the 1800s, but by the early 1900s the breeding range crashed due to changing habitats. It is thought that just 800–1,500 pairs nest in the United States in any given year, producing 4,000–4,500 kites at the end of the breeding season. Semisocial, with several individuals sharing the same territory.

Stunning in flight. Easily identified by its contrasting colors and forked tail. Feeds during flight. Also drinks on the wing, skimming across the water like a swallow. Soars with wings flat, riding thermals high into the air. Rarely hovers like other raptors. An agile flier, collecting sticks for its nest much like the Osprey (pg. 169), breaking off sticks from dead trees with its feet during flight. One study estimated that over 200 items, such as twigs and pine needle sprigs, all carried singly, were used to build a nest.

Majority of the diet includes bees, butterflies, dragonflies and beetles, which are caught and eaten in flight. Will also snatch lizards and large insects, such as cicadas, from leaves of trees.

male

YEAR-ROUND
WINTER

Sharp-shinned Hawk
Accipiter striatus

HAWKS

Family: Hawks, Eagles and Kites (Accipitridae)

Size: M 9–11" (23–28 cm); WS 20–22" (50–56 cm)
F 11–13" (28–33 cm); WS 23–26" (58–66 cm)

Weight: 3½–5 oz. (99–142 g)

Male: A small woodland hawk with a tiny round head. Bluish gray back and head. Rusty red horizontal barring on a white chest. Long squared-off tail. Several dark tail bands, widest band at the end. Large orange-to-red eyes. Short yellow legs and long thin toes. In flight, the head barely projects past the bend of wings (wrists), which are often thrust forward.

Female: same as male, noticeably larger, up to one-third more than the male, with a gray back

Juvenile: same size as adults, with a brown back, heavy vertical streaking on the chest, bright yellow-to-orange eyes

Habitat: wooded backyards, woodlands, forests, parks

Food: small birds, small animals, reptiles, amphibians

Sounds: screams a high-pitched, whistle-like repetitive call when interlopers get close to the nest; can be very vocal during breeding season

Compare: Cooper's Hawk (pg. 109) is larger, has a larger head, smaller eyes, longer legs, slightly longer neck and a rounded tip of tail. During flight, the head of the Sharp-shinned does not protrude as far as the Cooper's. Red-shouldered Hawk (pg. 117) has a reddish head and belly and lacks a grayish back. Look for the squared tip of tail to help identify the Sharp-shinned Hawk.

Flight: short rounded wings and long narrow tail; head does not extend beyond the bend in wrist; fast, shallow wing beats interspersed with short gliding; soars in groups during migration on rising columns of warm air

Migration: complete to non-migrator, to southern states, Mexico and Central America

Nesting: platform, in a mature tree in thick deciduous woods, usually in the first fork or crotch near the main trunk, made of sticks, twigs and branches with green leaves; female builds a new nest or repairs an old one with new material; 1 brood

Eggs/Incubation: 4–5 white eggs with brown markings; female incubates 32–35 days; male does the most hunting and feeds the nesting female before and after the young hatch

Fledging: 24–27 days; female feeds the young; male does the majority of hunting and brings food to the female, who feeds the chicks; upon leaving the nest (fledging), the young still beg for food; chicks learn to hunt by watching and copying the behavior of the parents and are hunting by the end of their first summer; young migrate on their own, separate from the adults

Stan's Notes: This is a common small hawk that often can be seen swooping down on birds at your feeders. Its short rounded wings and long tail allow it to navigate through thick stands of trees during fast pursuit of prey. Common name comes from the sharp keel on the leading edge of its "shin," although it is actually below rather than above the bird's ankle on the tarsus bone of the foot. The tarsus in most birds is round.

The smallest of the American accipiters. Its head is so small that its eyes appear large, even though they are about the same size as those of Cooper's Hawk (pg. 109). A true bird hunter. Of all accipiters, it takes more birds than other types of prey.

Juveniles migrate weeks before the adults each fall. Although often seen in groups during migration, Sharp-shins migrate alone during the day, hunting for food early in the morning before the thermals start building in late morning.

Courtship is usually near the nest site. Pairs fly in circles, call to one another and land beside each other on a branch.

light morph

Short-tailed Hawk

Buteo brachyurus

YEAR-ROUND
SUMMER
WINTER

Family: Hawks, Eagles and Kites (Accipitridae)

Size: L 14–17" (36–43 cm); WS 3–3½' (.9–1.1 m)

Weight: 13–15 oz. (369–425 g)

Male: A stocky-bodied hawk with two color morphs. Very broad wings. Gray tail with many narrow bands and a dark terminal band. **Light morph** has a white belly, chest and chin, with a uniform dark head, back and tail. Head appears hooded. White leading half of wings and gray trailing half, with nearly black tips of primary flight feathers. **Dark morph** is uniform dark brown to nearly black overall except for yellow cere, legs and feet. Dark leading half of wings and gray trailing half with a dark terminal edge.

Female: same as male of the same morph

Juvenile: similar to adults of the same morph

Habitat: thick forests, woodlots, mangrove forests, rural to urban areas

Food: small to medium-sized birds, small reptiles and amphibians, small mammals

Sounds: screams a long, high-pitched clear "keeee" with a slight slur at the end; vocalizes mainly at the nest when disturbed by intruders; also vocalizes during courtship and when mate brings in food for young; young repeat a begging call

Compare: Broad-winged Hawk (pg. 113) has a rusty bib and wide tail bands. Use range to help identify Short-tailed Hawk.

adult light

adult dark

juvenile light

dark morph

juvenile dark

juvenile light

juvenile dark

Flight: very broad wings; rapid wing beats to gain altitude interspersed with long gliding; spends a lot of time soaring, gliding, parachuting and kiting; circles high up, stalling in the wind while searching for prey

Migration: partial to non-migrator, moving out of central Florida during autumn to southern Florida for the winter

Nesting: platform, near a main tree trunk or near the center in a pine, cypress or palm; male supplies nesting materials and female builds a large nest with sticks, twigs and branches and lines it with finer materials such as evergreen tree needles or green deciduous leaves; 1 brood

Eggs/Incubation: 2 (rarely 3) white eggs, occasionally with brown markings; female and male incubate 32–34 days; if both eggs hatch, usually only one survives; male hunts the most and feeds the nesting female before and after the young hatch

Fledging: 35–45 days; female feeds the young; male does the majority of hunting and brings food to the female, who feeds the chicks; upon leaving the nest (fledging), the young still continue to beg for food; chicks learn to hunt by copying the parents and are hunting by the end of their first summer

Stan's Notes: An uncommon bird found primarily in Florida; occasionally seen in the southern tip of Texas. Exact numbers in Florida are unknown, but there are probably fewer than 500. A shy forest hawk that lives in inaccessible habitat. With the rapidly changing habitats in southern Florida, this species may be pushed out.

Usually hunts on the wing, with Red-winged Blackbirds and meadowlarks making up most of the bird diet. Feeds while perched; sometimes swallows prey whole during flight.

Spends much time soaring and riding thermals high in the sky. When it sees prey, it dives like a falcon in a long vertical dive, periodically stalling, pulling up, then diving again. Near the end of the dive it parachutes onto the prey directly from above, thus taking it by surprise. Rarely, if ever, hovers.

During winter it can be found in open forests. Sometimes seen in suburban areas and business parks that support some of its habitat. During breeding season it is often deep in thick forests, making it difficult to find.

Gray Hawk

Asturina nitida

Family: Hawks, Eagles and Kites (Accipitridae)

Size: L 15–18" (38–45 cm); WS 32–38" (80–96 cm)

Weight: 13–23 oz. (369–652 g)

Male: An all-gray hawk with a large body and wide wings. Light gray barring on chest, extending onto the legs. White lower belly and several distinctive black and white tail bands. Distinctive white U mark at base of tail when viewed from above. Dark tips of wings (primaries). Wing tips on perched birds are much shorter than tip of tail, revealing much of the tail. Yellow base of bill (cere). Short dark bill. Yellow legs and feet.

Female: same as male, slightly larger

Juvenile: thick dark eye line, dark malar on white cheeks, brown head, nape, back and upper wings, white breast and belly with many dark spots, brown rump, long tail with fine bands

Habitat: wooded hills, along streams and rivers, riparian areas with cottonwoods and other tall trees

Food: reptiles, small mammals, small birds, fish, large insects

Sounds: series of long descending whistles, often a series of 3–4 at a time

Compare: Smaller than the Zone-tailed Hawk (pg. 129), which is nearly black and has two-toned wings, as seen in flight. Common Black-Hawk (pg. 145) is black with a short wide tail and single white tail band. Gray Hawk is the only all-gray hawk that resides in the southern tip of Texas.

Flight: slow, buoyant wing beats interspersed with short gliding; holds wings straight out; sometimes circles high up

Migration: non-migrator; moves around in winter to find food

Nesting: platform, in a large mature sycamore or cottonwood tree; male and female build a large nest with green sticks, twigs and branches and line it with finer green branches with leaves or needles; 1 brood

Eggs/Incubation: 1–3 white-to-pale blue eggs; female incubates 30–34 days; male does the most hunting and feeds the nesting female before and after the young hatch

Fledging: 30–35 days; female feeds the young; male does the majority of hunting and brings food to the female, who feeds the chicks; the young continue to beg for food after fledging; chicks learn to hunt by watching and copying their parents and are hunting by the end of their first summer

Stan's Notes: This is a large-bodied hawk with broad wings, similar to the Broad-winged Hawk (pg. 113) of the eastern United States. Lives in valleys with cottonwoods and other tall trees growing by streams and rivers. Common in Mexico, with range extending into the extreme southern tip of Texas, where it can be seen year-round.

Often perches in open spaces while hunting for reptiles and small mammals, quickly flying down to snatch prey. Mainly feeds on a wide variety of snakes and other reptiles. Fairly easy to identify since it is uniform gray with a distinctive white U on top of the tail at the base, as seen from above.

A monogamous hawk and solitary nester. In spring it performs an aerial courtship display, with the male chasing the female, spiraling and looping while calling. Once mated, the calling decreases and nest construction begins. Nests are located high up and are well concealed in tall trees along streams. Nests are often reused year after year. Pairs will bring in new nesting material each season to add to the old nest.

Cooper's Hawk

Accipiter cooperii

YEAR-ROUND
WINTER

Family: Hawks, Eagles and Kites (Accipitridae)

Size: M 14–16" (36–40 cm); WS 28–30" (71–76 cm)
F 16–19" (40–48 cm); WS 31–34" (79–86 cm)

Weight: 12–16 oz. (340–454 g)

Male: Medium hawk with a blue-gray head, neck, back and upperwings. Rusty red horizontal barring on a white breast. Large squared head. Dark crown. Orange-to-red eyes. Long tail, rounded tip (terminal) with a few dark bands and wide light band. In flight, head projects well past the wrists, which are usually not thrust forward. Long yellow legs and feet.

Female: similar to male, noticeably larger, up to one-third more than the male, with a gray back

Juvenile: brown head and back, vertical brown streaks on a white breast, pale yellow eyes

Habitat: woodlands, forests, wooded backyards, parks

Food: small birds, mammals, reptiles, amphibians

Sounds: screams a repetitive nasal "cack-cack-cack-cack" call when trespassers are near the nest; can be very vocal during breeding season

Compare: Larger than the Sharp-shinned Hawk (pg. 97), with a larger head, darker cap, longer legs and rounded tail, not a squared tail. Unlike Sharp-shinned, Cooper's wings are perpendicular to the body, usually not thrust forward in flight. Eyes look smaller than those of Sharp-shinned, but only because the Cooper's head is so much larger. Juvenile Cooper's has pale yellow eyes, not bright yellow eyes like the juvenile Sharp-shinned.

adult

adult dorsal

juvenile

juvenile dorsal

juvenile

Flight: stubby rounded wings, long tail and large head; head projects beyond the bend in wings; long glides followed by a few quick flaps; soars in groups during migration on rising columns of warm air

Migration: partial to non-migrator; northern birds move south to join resident birds for the winter

Nesting: platform, in a medium to large tree in dense deciduous woods, usually in the first fork or crotch of a tree near the main trunk, constructed with sticks, twigs and branches with green leaves still attached; repairs an old nest or male and female build a new nest each year; 1 brood

Eggs/Incubation: 2–4 greenish eggs with brown markings; female and male incubate 32–36 days; male does the most hunting and feeds the nesting female before and after the young hatch

Fledging: 28–32 days; male and female feed young; male does the majority of hunting and brings food to the female, who feeds the chicks; upon leaving the nest (fledging), the young continue to beg for food; chicks learn to hunt by watching and copying parental behavior and are hunting by the end of their first summer, before they migrate

Stan's Notes: One of the most common woodland hawks, found throughout the South. Its short rounded wings help it maneuver among trees while pursuing small birds. Most of the hawks seen chasing birds around your bird feeder are Cooper's Hawks. Ambushes backyard feeders, hunting for unsuspecting birds. Known to chase small birds into picture windows, picking up stunned birds from the ground. Will also fly into heavy brush or even run on the ground in pursuit of birds that are hidden in thick cover. Once called Chicken Hawk for its habit of taking chickens from farms.

Nestlings have gray eyes that turn pale yellow at 1 year of age and become dark red later, after 3–5 years. Noting the color of the eyes is not an accurate way to determine age. Adult males obtain red eyes sooner than females, but some females never obtain dark red eyes. The dark cap is another sign of a mature or adult bird, but this is also not a good way to estimate age.

Broad-winged Hawk

Buteo platypterus

SUMMER
WINTER

Family: Hawks, Eagles and Kites (Accipitridae)

Size: L 14–19" (36–48 cm); WS 30–36" (76–91 cm)

Weight: 10–17 oz. (284–482 g)

Male: Brown-to-tan head, back and upperwings. Thick, rusty horizontal bars or V-shaped markings on the breast. Most have a solid rusty brown breast, forming a bib. Eyes brown to pale orange. Short wide wings. White underwings, black "finger-tips" (primaries) and a dark trailing edge. Rusty brown axillaries. Wide dark subterminal tail band with a white edge. This species has a dark morph, but it is very uncommon; overall dark brown with 2 wide black tail bands and a white band in between.

Female: same as male, slightly larger

Juvenile: vertical brown streaks on the breast and belly, narrow dusky gray band on the trailing edge of wings, numerous narrow gray tail bands

Habitat: forests, woodlands, wooded backyards, parks

Food: snakes, frogs, toads, small birds, small mammals, large insects

Sounds: repeats a high-pitched, whistle-like screaming call when intruders are close to the nest

Compare: Similar size as Red-shouldered Hawk (pg. 117), but lacks the rufous shoulders and white spots on wings and back. Cooper's Hawk (pg. 109) has a gray back, rusty chest and belly and longer, narrower tail. Look for the rusty brown bib on the breast to help identify the Broad-winged Hawk.

adult

adult dorsal

juvenile

juvenile

adult dark

Flight: large barrel-shaped body, relatively short tail and broad wings, wider at the center with rounded wing tips and short "fingertips" (primaries); shallow, rapid wing beats interspersed with short to long gliding; during migration, soars in groups (kettles) on rising columns of warm air

Migration: complete migrator, to the southern tip of Florida, southern Mexico, Central and South America

Nesting: platform, in a mature tree in dense deciduous woods, usually in the first fork or crotch, constructed with sticks, twigs and branches with green leaves still attached; female and male construct a new nest each year or repair an old nest, bringing in new nesting material; 1 brood

Eggs/Incubation: 2–3 off-white eggs with brown markings; female incubates 28–32 days; male does the most hunting and feeds the nesting female before and after the young hatch

Fledging: 34–40 days; female and male feed young; male does the most hunting and brings food to the female, who feeds the chicks; upon leaving the nest (fledging), young beg for food, chasing their parents after they capture prey; chicks watch the parents hunt and are hunting by the end of their first summer

Stan's Notes: A forest buteo hawk, common in the South. Often heard before seen when disturbed around the nest. Can be aggressive near the nest, dive-bombing human trespassers. Spends most of its time perching, hunting for small birds, snakes and frogs in dense woodlands. Its short rounded wings help it maneuver safely in thick forests. Sky-dance courtship flights include steep closed-wing dives, terminating with a sharp upward flight, rolling over and flying upside down. Often very vocal during courtship.

A highly migratory hawk and the most abundant migrating hawk species at hawk watch locations every fall. Seen in large clusters during fall and spring migration, swirling in tight groups known as kettles. Very punctual during migration, with juvenile birds moving through the South in large groups in early September, followed by adults mid-month. By the second week of October most have moved through.

Also called Broadwing or Broadie, and Aguililla Alas Anchas or Aguililla Aluda in Spanish. The dark morph of this species is extremely uncommon in the South.

Southern

Red-shouldered Hawk

Buteo lineatus

Family: Hawks, Eagles and Kites (Accipitridae)

Size: L 15–19" (38–48 cm); WS 3–3½' (.9–1.1 m)

Weight: 10–17 oz. (284–482 g)

Male: A medium-sized hawk with a cinnamon (rufous) head, shoulders, breast and belly. Upperwings and back are dark brown to nearly black, with white spots covering upperwings. Long rounded tail has thin, light tail bands alternating with wide black bands. Rufous wing linings (underwing coverts), obvious during flight.

Female: same as male, slightly larger

Juvenile: similar to adults, lacks the rusty red color, has a white breast with dark vertical streaking and several narrow bands on the tail

Habitat: wooded backyards, forests, woodlands, parks, roadsides

Food: reptiles, amphibians, large insects, small birds

Sounds: very vocal; repeats a distinctive, high-pitched clear whistle or screaming call when interlopers get near the nest and during breeding season

Compare: Cooper's Hawk (pg. 109) also has a rufous breast and belly, but is overall thinner and has a much longer tail. Broad-winged Hawk (pg. 113) lacks the rusty red wing linings. Red-tailed Hawk (pg. 153) is larger and has a white breast.

adult Eastern

adult Florida

juvenile Eastern

adult Florida

juvenile Eastern

Eastern

juvenile Eastern

juvenile Florida

mother and chicks

Flight: long broad wings, wider at the center, with rounded wing tips, short "fingertips" (primaries) and a white crescent-shaped pattern across the base of the wing tips; tail relatively short and wide; flaps with fast, stiff wing beats alternating with a gliding pattern; soars in groups during migration on rising columns of warm air

Migration: non-migrator to partial; moves around in winter to find food

Nesting: platform, in a mature tree in dense deciduous woods, usually in the first fork or crotch near the main trunk, made with sticks, twigs and branches that have green leaves attached; female and male repair an old nest or build a new nest each year; 1 brood

Eggs/Incubation: 2–4 white eggs with dark markings; female and male incubate 27–29 days; male does the most hunting and feeds the nesting female before and after the young hatch

Fledging: 39–45 days; female feeds the young; male does the majority of hunting and brings food to the female, who feeds the chicks; upon leaving the nest (fledging), the young still beg for food; chicks learn to hunt by copying the parents' behavior and are hunting by the end of their first summer

Stan's Notes: A woodland hawk found in woodsy backyards and parks in southern states. Tolerates the presence of people well. Likes to hunt forest edges, spotting frogs, snakes, insects, an occasional bird and other prey while perching.

Adults return to the same nest and territory for many years; the young also return. Starts nest building in February, with young leaving the nest by June. Matures sexually at 2–3 years of age.

Two groups of hawks—buteos and accipiters. Buteos, such as Red-tailed Hawks (pg. 153), are open country hawks. Accipiters, such as the Sharp-shinned Hawk (pg. 97) and Cooper's Hawk (pg. 109), are woodland hawks. The Red-shouldered Hawk is unique because it is a forest buteo that is more closely related to Red-tailed Hawks (which hunt in open country) than it is to the forest-dwelling Sharp-shinned and Cooper's Hawks.

At least four races (subspecies) are found in North America— Southern, Eastern, Florida and California (not shown). Like Red-tailed Hawks, the Red-shouldered is one of the few hawk species with different color variations (subspecies) in different parts of the country.

male

Northern Harrier

Circus cyaneus

YEAR-ROUND
SUMMER
WINTER

Family: Hawks, Eagles and Kites (Accipitridae)

Size: M 16–18" (40–45 cm); WS 3¼–3½' (1–1.1 m)
F 18–20" (45–50 cm); WS 3½–4' (1.1–1.2 m)

Weight: 12–15 oz. (340–425 g)

Male: Light gray head and silver gray back and upper-wings. White underwings, belly and large rump patch. Faint streaking on chest. Faint tail bands. Black wing tips and black trailing edge of wings. Owl-like facial disks. Yellow eyes and dark bill.

Female: noticeably larger than the male, head and back are dark to rusty brown, vertical brown streaks on chest and belly, large white rump patch, thin black bands on tail, owl-like facial disks, yellow eyes, small dark bill

Juvenile: similar to the adult female, orange breast without vertical streaks, eyes are dark brown to tan

Habitat: open fields, marshes, wetlands, meadows, parks

Food: small mammals, snakes, insects, small birds

Sounds: usually silent; gives a short high-pitched whistle; repeats a sharp call when trespassers come near the nest

Compare: Slimmer and has a longer tail than Red-tailed Hawk (pg. 153). Turkey Vulture (pg. 177) shares a similar tilting flight pattern, but it is much larger, darker and lacks the white rump patch. Short-eared Owl (pg. 213) shares the facial disks and has a similar characteristic low flight pattern, but the Harrier has a longer tail and white rump patch. Look for the black tail bands, white rump patch and characteristic flight to help identify.

male

female

juvenile

juvenile

female

Flight: slim body; characteristic low flight, gliding just above the ground, often under 10' (3 m); deep wing beats interspersed with short gliding; series of flapping and gliding permit it to follow land contours and drop suddenly onto prey; holds wings horizontally and slightly above the body, tilting back and forth in the wind similar to the Turkey Vulture (pg. 177)

Migration: complete migrator, moving out of northern states and into southern states for the winter

Nesting: ground nest, sometimes low in a shrub, flimsy nest built with grass and sticks; female builds a new nest each year with some help from the male; 1 brood

Eggs/Incubation: 4–8 bluish white eggs, small percentage have brown markings; female incubates 31–32 days; male does the most hunting and feeds the nesting female before and after the young hatch

Fledging: 30–35 days; female feeds the young; male does the majority of hunting and brings food to the female, who feeds the chicks; upon leaving the nest (fledging), the young still continue to beg for food; chicks learn how to hunt by watching and copying their parents' behavior and are hunting by the end of the first summer

Stan's Notes: A slim-bodied, long-tailed raptor. One of the easiest hawks to identify simply by its characteristic low flight pattern. Harriers glide just aboveground, usually under 10 feet (3 m), following the contours of land while searching for prey, then dropping suddenly onto prey. Holds wings in a horizontal position just above the level of the body when in flight. Often tilts back and forth in the wind, similar to the way vultures fly.

Regardless of its age, the Northern Harrier has distinctive owl-like facial disks. When hunting, uses its excellent hearing with the aid of the facial disks to detect the presence of prey before spotting it. Hunts by ambush, flying suddenly over a reptile, small bird, mouse or other small animal and dropping out of the sky onto the prey.

Formerly called Marsh Hawk due to its habit of hunting over marshes. Feeds and nests on the ground. Will perch on the ground to preen, rest and sleep.

YEAR-ROUND

White-tailed Hawk

Buteo albicaudatus

Family: Hawks, Eagles and Kites (Accipitridae)

Size: L 18–21" (45–53 cm); WS 3¾–4½' (1.14–1.4 m)

Weight: 2–2½ lb. (.9–1.1 kg)

Male: Stocky-bodied with light gray on the head, back and wings and a rufous patch on the shoulders. White chin, breast and belly. Yellow cere, legs and feet. When perched, wing tips extend well beyond the tail. White breast blends into a white leading half of wings, seen in flight; trailing half of wings is dark with dark wing tips (primaries) A very short, wide white tail with a single dark subterminal band.

Female: same as male, slightly larger

Juvenile: similar to adults, but has a dark belly and chin and lacks the obvious light gray; individuals are highly variable, with light, moderate or heavy markings; takes 3 years to reach maturity and obtain adult plumage

Habitat: coastal savannas, open scrublands, rural to urban areas

Food: small mammals and birds, small reptiles and amphibians, insects

Sounds: high-pitched laughing call, given repeatedly

Compare: Swainson's Hawk (pg. 141) has a rusty bib and brown back and upper surface of wings. In flight the Swainson's bib is clearly visible and its dark trailing half of wings is darker and more pronounced than that of White-tailed. Wide wings, thick body and extremely short tail help to identify the White-tailed.

adult

adult dorsal

juvenile

juvenile

Flight: wide wings with four noticeable "fingertips"; rapid and full wing beats to gain altitude interspersed with long periods of soaring; soaring, gliding and riding thermals takes up much of the flight time; circles high up before moving away and out of sight

Migration: non-migrator; year-round resident in far southern and southeastern Texas

Nesting: platform, directly on top of tree or at the center; female and male build a nest with sticks, twigs and branches and line it with finer materials; 1 brood

Eggs/Incubation: 1–4 white eggs, sometimes spotted with brown; female and male incubate 30–31 days; male does the most hunting and feeds the nesting female before and after the young hatch

Fledging: 45–50 days; female feeds the young; male does the majority of hunting and brings food to the female, who feeds the chicks; upon leaving the nest (fledging), the young still continue to beg for food; chicks learn to hunt by watching their parents and are hunting by the end of their first summer

Stan's Notes: An uncommon species found only in southern Texas and extending south through most of Mexico. This is a tropical hawk that also resides in Central and South America. Only small trees grow in their range, so nests are often in the tallest tree around and only 15 feet (4.6 m) or so off the ground.

Inhabits open grassy and shrubby habitat. Often attracted to natural fires to take advantage of fleeing animals.

Hunts by hovering or kiting before plunging down onto prey. Will often feed on the ground or move to a nearby tree. Hunts mainly small mammals, such as rabbits and rats, but also takes many reptiles and even amphibians. Will also take larger insects such as grasshoppers and beetles.

Unlike other species of hawks, its wing tips extend well beyond the tail, up to several inches longer. It has four primary flight feathers ("fingertips"), which can be seen in flight. Only the Swainson's Hawk (pg. 141) and Broad-winged Hawk (pg. 113) share this characteristic; all other buteos have five. This often makes the wing tips look longer, narrower and more pointed.

Zone-tailed Hawk

Buteo albonotatus

MIGRATION
SUMMER

Family: Hawks, Eagles and Kites (Accipitridae)

Size: L 18–22" (45–56 cm); WS 4–4½' (1.2–1.4 m)

Weight: 1¼–2½ lb. (.6–1.1 kg)

Male: A strikingly dark hawk, nearly overall black, with a wide white tail band and several thin tail bands. Belly and wing linings are black, as seen in flight. Gray trailing half of wings with a black edge. Pale yellow skin at the base of bill (cere). Dark eyes.

Female: same as male, slightly larger

Juvenile: similar to adults, gray flecks on chest, fine gray barring on trailing half of wings and tail, lacks distinctive tail bands

Habitat: open fields, meadows, along highways, parks, rural areas

Food: reptiles, amphibians, birds, small and medium-sized mammals

Sounds: screams a long high-pitched whistle like that of a Red-tailed Hawk (pg. 153); young repeat a very high-pitched begging call for food

Compare: Very similar to the Turkey Vulture (pg. 177), which is larger and shares the two-toned wings, but has a naked red head and lacks the tail bands. Common Black-Hawk (pg. 145) is similar in size and color, but has much wider wings, a shorter tail and wider tail band.

adult

juvenile

Flight: deep, slow wing beats interspersed with long gliding; circles high up, stalling in wind while searching for prey, holds wings in a deep angle (dihedral), very similar to Turkey Vulture (pg. 177), teetering back and forth from wing tip to wing tip

Migration: complete migrator, to Mexico, Central and South America

Nesting: platform, in a large mature tree; male and female construct a large nest with sticks, twigs and branches and line it with finer materials such as evergreen tree needles or green deciduous leaves; 1 brood

Eggs/Incubation: 2–3 white eggs with lavender-to-brown markings; female and male incubate 30–35 days; male hunts the most and feeds the nesting female

Fledging: 45–46 days; female feeds the young; male does the most hunting and brings food to the female, who feeds the chicks; upon leaving the nest (fledging), the young continue to beg for food; chicks learn to hunt by watching and copying their parents and are hunting by the end of their first summer

Stan's Notes: A unique hawk that looks like a vulture and is often with vultures. Unlike vultures, however, it is an efficient predator. Mimics vultures, flying in circles, swirling around, soaring on thermals while looking for reptiles, amphibians, small mammals and birds to drop down on suddenly and grab. Sometimes will take small birds while in flight.

Even a trained eye can be confused by this vulture look-alike. Turkey Vulture (pg. 177), however, is much more common than Zone-tailed, which has a relatively limited range and is not very common. Range extends from Arizona to western Texas, south to Brazil, Bolivia and Argentina. Migrates out of the United States in winter; sometimes wanders out of its normal range.

Well known for its spectacular courtship displays, with pairs performing aerial loops, dives and rolls, reaching heights of 150–200 feet (50–60 m). Most displays take place over the nesting area. Both male and female aggressively guard the nest site.

Doesn't have a light morph, like most other buteo species. Also called Black Buzzard and Zone-tailed Buzzard. Common name "Buzzard" is usually reserved for raptors in the Old World and is not typically used in North America.

Harris's Hawk

Parabuteo unicinctus

Family: Hawks, Eagles and Kites (Accipitridae)

Size: L 18–22" (45–56 cm); WS 3¾–4' (1.14–1.2 m)

Weight: 1½–2½ lb. (.7–1.1 kg)

Male: Overall dark brown. Distinctive rusty brown shoulders, wing linings and feathers on legs. Black tail with a bright white tip. Bright white rump. Large yellow patch (cere) at base of bill. Long yellow legs and yellow feet. Rusty wing linings, seen in flight.

Female: same as male, slightly larger

Juvenile: overall lighter brown than the adults, white streaks on the breast, brown tail

Habitat: desert scrub, semiarid woodlands near water, city parks, suburban yards

Food: small to medium animals, snakes and other reptiles, small birds, amphibians, large insects

Sounds: screams a high-pitched, whistle-like repetitive call when intruders are near the nest; can be very vocal during breeding season

Compare: Red-tailed Hawk (pg. 153) has a white breast and lacks the rusty markings of the Harris's Hawk. Similar size as the light morph Swainson's Hawk (pg. 141), which has a white belly. The dark morph Swainson's has semi-rusty wing coverts and a dark body, but lacks the bright white rump and tip of tail. The dark morph Ferruginous Hawk (pg. 157) has a white tail and trailing half of wings. Look for rusty markings on the shoulders, a white rump and white-tipped black tail to help identify the Harris's Hawk.

juvenile

juvenile

Flight: wide dark wings with rounded tips and rusty wing linings; shallow, rapid wing beats interspersed with short or long gliding; glides on slightly cupped wings and soars with wing tips upward (dihedral); hunts in small groups

Migration: non-migrator; moves around to find food

Nesting: platform, in a mature tree in dense deciduous woods, usually in the first fork or tree crotch, built with sticks, twigs and branches with green leaves; female and male build anew each year or repair an old nest with new materials; 1–2 broods

Eggs/Incubation: 3–4 pale white eggs with some brown markings; female and male incubate 33–36 days; male does the most hunting and feeds the nesting female, sometimes sharing duties with other young male family members

Fledging: 43–49 days; female and male feed young; male does the most hunting and brings food to the female, who feeds the chicks; the young still beg after fledging and chase their parents for food; parents feed the young for up to 6 months; chicks learn to hunt by watching and copying their parents and are hunting by the end of their first summer

Stan's Notes: Named after Edward Harris, a friend of John James Audubon. Formerly called Bay-winged Hawk, referring to its distinctive wing markings. Can be a rather tame hawk. Usually found in desert scrub and areas with tall trees for nesting, often near water. Not uncommon to see it in city parks and suburban yards. Now extinct in some areas and reintroduced in others such as southern California. Most stable populations are in southern Texas and southern Arizona.

Unlike most other raptors, hunts in small groups, usually family members. Cooperative hunting aids in the capture of larger prey such as jackrabbits. Family members stage atop cacti or shrubs as another flies to the ground and runs into thick brush, flushing out prey, while other hunting party members give chase on the wing. Captured prey is shared.

Young hatch up to a couple days apart. Young males often stay to help hunt and raise families. Common for up to three males to attend a female (polyandry) and help with child-rearing. Raises second broods in years with abundant food.

light morph

Rough-legged Hawk

Buteo lagopus

Family: Hawks, Eagles and Kites (Accipitridae)

Size: L 18–23" (45–58 cm); WS 4–4½' (1.2–1.4 m)

Weight: 2–2⅛ lb. (.9–1 kg)

Male: Large bird of prey, with two color morphs. Both morphs have a dark belly, axillaries and bill. Long white tail with a dark subterminal band and white tip. White rump patch. Feathered legs and small yellow feet. Relatively long wings with a dark band on the trailing edge. **Light morph** has white underwings and distinctive large dark wrist (carpal) marks. **Dark morph** has a brown-to-black body and wing linings (underwing coverts), with a light gray trailing half of wings.

Female: same as male, slightly larger

Juvenile: same as adult female, lacks a dark band on the trailing edge of wings and a dark subterminal tail band

Habitat: prairies, open fields, agricultural fields, large vacant lots, parks

Food: mice, voles and other small mammals

Sounds: often quiet; repeats a weak, simple high-pitched scream like that of Red-tailed Hawk (pg. 153)

Compare: The Red-tailed Hawk (pg. 153) lacks the large dark wrist marks and a subterminal tail band. The Osprey (pg. 169) has similar dark wrist marks, but it lacks a dark belly and is seen throughout the South at various times during the year. The Rough-legged is a winter visitor in some southern states, so take the range and season into account to help identify it.

adult light

juvenile light

dark morph

juvenile light dorsal

adult dark

juvenile light

juvenile dark

juvenile dark

Flight: relatively long wings and long tail; deep, full wing beats interspersed with short gliding; faces into strong wind and hovers, looking for prey; may pump its wings hard to stall flight for a short time when the wind is mild

Migration: complete migrator, to southern states during winter; moves around in groups of up to 10–25 individuals, remaining together all winter

Nesting: platform, on top of a small tree, on the edge of a cliff, constructed with sticks, twigs and branches, lined with grasses and feathers; female and male build a new nest each year or repair an old nest, adding new nesting material; 1 brood

Eggs/Incubation: 2–6 white eggs; female incubates 28–31 days; male does the most hunting and feeds the nesting female before and after the young hatch

Fledging: 39–43 days; female feeds the young; male does the majority of hunting and brings food to the female, who feeds the chicks; when the young leave the nest (fledge), they still continue to beg for food; chicks learn to hunt by watching and copying the behavior of their parents and are hunting by the end of their first summer

Stan's Notes: Named for the feathers on its legs. This hawk appears in two color morphs, light and dark. The light morph is more common, but both are seen together.

Nests in Canada's Northwest Territories and Alaska, moving down to the northern half of the country during winter. More numerous in some winters than in others. Can be seen in large numbers during fall and spring migration, but this hawk is not common in Gulf Coast states.

Almost always in groups of up to 10–25 birds, hunting in large open fields or prairies. Groups are mixed, consisting of adults and juveniles and light and dark morphs. Individuals try to steal from each other after one makes a kill. Monogamous, with pairs often staying together for life.

Has smaller, weaker feet than other raptors of similar size and must hunt smaller prey. Hunts from the air, often hovering, facing into a strong wind before diving for mice or voles. Will also perch in a tree or on a fence post to watch for prey when the wind is weak. Often feeds on the ground after catching prey. Perches on surprisingly thin branches at the top of small trees.

male light morph

MIGRATION
SUMMER

Swainson's Hawk

Buteo swainsoni

Family: Hawks, Eagles and Kites (Accipitridae)

Size: L 19–22" (48–56 cm); WS 4¼–4¾' (1.3–1.45 m)

Weight: 2–2¼ lb. (.9–1 kg)

Male: Extremely variable plumage, with three distinct color morphs. All morphs have a small yellow patch at the base of bill (cere), yellow legs and feet and dark brown eyes. When perched, wing tips extend just beyond the tail. **Light morph** is brown with a gray head, white belly, warm rusty breast (bib) and white face. **Intermediate morph** has a dark breast, rusty belly and white face. **Dark morph** is nearly all dark brown with a rusty color low on belly. Lacks a white face.

Female: similar to male, but has a dark brown head and upper breast (bib)

Juvenile: similar to adult of the same morph

Habitat: open country, fields, meadows, prairies, shelterbelts, roadsides

Food: small to medium animals, insects, snakes, birds

Sounds: screams a long, very high-pitched call like that of the Red-tailed Hawk (pg. 153), but higher in pitch and slightly longer

Compare: The Red-tailed Hawk (pg. 153) has a white breast and lacks a bib. Rough-legged (pg. 137) and Ferruginous Hawks (pg. 157) have lighter trailing edges of wings; also, underwings of the Ferruginous are nearly all white with rusty wing linings. Look for the long candlestick-shaped wings with a two-toned underwing pattern to help identify the Swainson's Hawk.

adult male light

adult dark

female light morph

juvenile light

juvenile light

juvenile dark

adult dark

adult intermediate

Flight: slender body with long candlestick-shaped wings and a two-toned underwing pattern; wings are slightly upturned in a flattened V position; series of strong, deep wing beats followed by long glides; soars in groups on rising columns of warm air during migration

Migration: complete migrator, to Central and South America

Nesting: platform, in a mature tree, a lone tree in open prairie or in a shelterbelt, often in the first fork or crotch of a tree, built with sticks, twigs and branches with green leaves still attached; female and male construct a new nest each year or repair an old nest, bringing in new nesting material; uses an old nest up to 50 percent of the time; 1 brood

Eggs/Incubation: 2–4 bluish or white eggs, some with brown markings; female and male incubate 28–35 days; male does the most hunting and feeds the nesting female before and after the young hatch

Fledging: 28–30 days; female and male feed young; male does the majority of hunting and brings food to the female, who feeds the chicks; when the young leave the nest (fledge), they continue to beg for food; chicks learn how to hunt by watching and copying their parents' behavior and are hunting by the end of the first summer

Stan's Notes: A slender, open country hawk. Hunts rabbits, insects, snakes and small birds when soaring (kiting) or perching. The light morph is the most common of the three color types; intermediate and dark morphs are less common.

Males perform aerial acrobatics to impress females. Maneuvers include soaring over the nest, diving up to 50 feet (15 m), rapid wing beats, vertical climbs into a stall and then diving again.

Even minor nest disturbance can cause nest failure. One study showed that as much as 30 percent of nest failures occur in shelterbelts. Shelterbelt nests are at higher risk due to hail, high winds and constant disturbance from agricultural activities.

Gathers in large flocks each fall for migration. Migrates during the daytime, using columns of warm rising air to gain altitude before gliding for long distances. Most will travel about 11,000–15,000 miles (17,710–24,150 km) on their annual migration to South America.

Common Black-Hawk

Buteogallus anthracinus

Family: Hawks, Eagles and Kites (Accipitridae)

Size: L 20–22" (50–56 cm); WS 3¼–4¼' (1–1.3 m)

Weight: 1½–3 lb. (.7–1.4 kg)

Male: A strikingly large-bodied dark hawk with a very short tail. Overall black with a wide white tail band near the base of tail and a very narrow terminal white band. Long yellow legs. Yellow skin at base of bill (cere). Dark eyes. Very broad wings with blunt round tips. Appears all black in flight, with a comma-shaped pale gray mark near the wrists (carpal). Top surface of wings is tinged brown with a distinct black trailing edge.

Female: same as male, slightly larger

Juvenile: similar to adults, with speckled wings and tail and large pale white panels on each wing, many wavy narrow tail bands

Habitat: almost always associated with water, such as rivers, and other riparian areas with tall trees such as cottonwoods

Food: amphibians, reptiles, crayfish, fish, crabs, small mammals, large insects

Sounds: series of high sharp whistles and screams that increase in intensity when disturbed, then trail off; often calls when soaring or while displaying for its mate during the breeding season

Compare: Zone-tailed Hawk (pg. 129) has a longer tail and lacks the carpal mark. Turkey Vulture (pg. 177) has two-toned wings, a naked red head and longer tail.

Flight: deep, slow, smooth wing beats interspersed with long gliding; circles high up while searching for prey; holds wings flat and steady during soaring

Migration: complete migrator; moves out of the United States during fall; winters in Mexico and Central and South America

Nesting: platform, in a large mature tree such as cottonwood or sycamore; male and female build a large nest with sticks, twigs and branches and line it with finer materials such as green deciduous leaves; 1 brood

Eggs/Incubation: 1–3 white eggs with small brown marks; female and male incubate 32–36 days; male does the most hunting and feeds the nesting female before and after the young hatch

Fledging: 42–47 days; female feeds the young; male does the majority of hunting and brings food to the female, who feeds the chicks; upon leaving the nest (fledging), the young still continue to beg for food; chicks learn to hunt by watching and copying parental behavior and are hunting by the end of their first summer

Stan's Notes: The Common Black-Hawk is not that common in the United States, but it can be very common in Mexico and Central and South America.

Usually associated with water, such as rivers, where it hunts amphibians and reptiles while perching in nearby trees. Prefers crabs, however, as its main food source where it can find them. Also takes crayfish and fish, both of which aren't very common food items for hawks.

Appears all black in flight, with an extremely short tail and a single wide white band near the base. Its very long yellow legs, also seen in flight, are also unique to this species.

Monogamous and nests alone. Vulnerable to nest disturbance and will abandon the nest when there is too much activity.

American Goshawk

Accipiter gentilis

Family: Hawks, Eagles and Kites (Accipitridae)

Size: M 18–20" (45–50 cm); WS 3¼–3½' (1–1.1 m)
F 21–25" (53–64 cm); WS 3½–3¾' (1.1–1.14 m)

Weight: M 1½–1¾ lb. (.7–.8 kg); F 1¾–2 lb. (.8–.9 kg)

Male: A large hawk with a bluish gray back and upper wings. Light gray breast and belly with fine horizontal barring. Gray underwings with fine dark barring. Prominent white eyebrows (superciliary lines). Long gray tail with fluffy white undertail coverts. Black crown and line through the eyes. Deep red-to-mahogany eyes. Yellow feet.

Female: similar to male, noticeably larger, barring on the breast is more coarse

Juvenile: overall brown with vertical streaks on the chest, irregular dark bands on the tail, yellow eyes

Habitat: woodlands, forests, wooded backyards, parks

Food: small mammals (especially Snowshoe Hares), small and large birds (especially Ruffed Grouse)

Sounds: high-pitched repetitive "kee-kee-kee" similar to the call of the Cooper's Hawk (pg. 109) when intruders get near the nest

Compare: Larger than Cooper's Hawk (pg. 109), which lacks white superciliary lines and has a rusty chest. Much larger than Sharp-shinned Hawk (pg. 97), which has a rusty breast. Look for the gray breast and fluffy white undertail coverts to help identify the Northern Goshawk.

adult

adult dorsal

juvenile

juvenile dorsal

juvenile

juvenile

Flight: large-bodied hawk with very long, wide wings, rounded wing tips, short "fingertips" (primaries) and a long narrow tail; rapid, shallow wing beats interspersed with short gliding; typical accipiter flight

Migration: non-migrator to irruptive; moves into midwestern and eastern states in 10-year cycles; moves around in winter

Nesting: platform, in a mature tree in dense deciduous forest or coniferous woods, usually in the first fork or crotch of a tree, constructed with sticks, twigs and branches with evergreen needles attached; male and female repair an old nest or build a new one; 1 brood

Eggs/Incubation: 2–5 bluish white eggs, sometimes with brown markings; female does most of the incubating 36–38 days; male does the hunting and feeds the nesting female before and after the young hatch

Fledging: 35–42 days; female feeds the young; male does the hunting and brings food to the female, who feeds the chicks; upon leaving the nest (fledging), the young continue to beg for food, chasing parents around after they capture prey; chicks learn to hunt by watching and copying parental behavior and are hunting by the end of their first summer

Stan's Notes: The largest and most aggressive of the three woodland accipiters. Hunts by chasing or surprising prey. This hawk is extremely dependent on the Snowshoe Hare for food. Goshawk populations are known to follow hare populations, irrupting out of normal range during the years when hare populations are low. This occurs in 10-year cycles. Also feeds on Ruffed Grouse as a secondary food source.

The smaller male is more agile than the female and hunts for smaller prey. The female hunts for larger prey. Female is very aggressive at the nest, boldly attacking intruders, even humans.

Usually starts to breed at 3 years of age. A small percentage will nest at 1–2 years of age without full adult plumage. During irruption years, juveniles migrate first, followed a couple weeks later by adults.

Eastern

Red-tailed Hawk

Buteo jamaicensis

YEAR-ROUND
WINTER

Family: Hawks, Eagles and Kites (Accipitridae)

Size: M 18–22" (45–56 cm); WS 3¾–4¼' (1.14–1.3 m)
F 19–25" (48–64 cm); WS 4¼–4¾' (1.3–1.45 m)

Weight: M 1¾–2 lb. (.8–.9 kg); F 2–2½ lb. (.9–1.1 kg)

Male: Five varieties, from chocolate brown to nearly all white. Overall brown with a lighter brown head (sometimes blond), white chest and a distinctive brown belly band. White V on the back (scapulars), seen when perched. Rusty red tail, usually seen only from above. White underwings with a small dark patch on the leading edge close to the shoulder (patagial). Heavy bill. White chin. Brown eyes and bright yellow cere

Female: same as male, noticeably larger

Juvenile: similar to adults, lacks the red tail, longer tail with narrow light and dark tail bands, speckled breast, dark belly band, light yellow eyes

Habitat: open fields, meadows, along highways, forests, wooded backyards, parks, rural to urban areas

Food: small and medium-sized mammals, large birds, snakes, fish, large insects, bats, carrion

Sounds: screams a long high-pitched call that falls in pitch and intensity when interlopers get close to the nest; young repeat a begging call for food

Compare: Red-shouldered Hawk (pg. 117) lacks a red tail and white breast. Cooper's Hawk (pg. 109) is smaller, with shorter, rounded wings.

adult Eastern

juvenile Harlan's

adult Harlan's

adult Krider's

juvenile Eastern

adult Krider's

adult Krider's

Eastern

juvenile Eastern

juvenile Harlan's

Flight: deep, slow wing beats interspersed with long gliding; circles high up, stalling in wind while searching for prey

Migration: partial to non-migrator, moving out of northern regions during autumn, joining resident birds in the South and moving around in winter to find food

Nesting: platform, in a large mature tree; male and female build a large stick nest with sticks, twigs and branches and line it with finer materials such as evergreen tree needles or green deciduous leaves; 1 brood

Eggs/Incubation: 2–3 white eggs, occasionally with brown markings; female and male incubate 30–35 days; male does the most hunting and feeds the nesting female before and after the young hatch

Fledging: 45–46 days; female feeds the young; male does the majority of hunting and brings food to the female, who feeds the chicks; upon leaving the nest (fledging), the young still continue to beg for food; chicks learn to hunt by watching and copying parental behavior and are hunting by the end of their first summer

Stan's Notes: Five subspecies (races) of Red-tails. Eastern is overall brown with a brown belly band and white chin. Harlan's is dark to nearly black, has a white rump and lacks a red tail. Krider's is bright white, lacks a belly band and occurs in the Great Plains. Western (not shown) has a heavily streaked belly and brown chin. Southwestern (not shown) has a faint belly band and pale red tail. Many subspecies occur in the South but are misidentified due to confusion with other hawks.

By far the most common hawk of the South. Often perches on power lines, fences and trees. Nests are large and commonly seen near the trunks of trees.

Eats a wide variety of prey from mice to rabbits, ducks, fish, large insects, bats and even carrion. Look for it circling over open fields or roadsides, searching for prey.

Comes back to the same nest site each year, adding materials and repairing the nest. Nests alone in a fairly large territory. Monogamous, with a long-term mate. Develops the red tail in its second year.

light morph

YEAR-ROUND
WINTER

Ferruginous Hawk

Buteo regalis

Family: Hawks, Eagles and Kites (Accipitridae)

Size: M 20–25" (50–64 cm); WS 4½–4¾' (1.4–1.45 m)
F 23–28" (58–71 cm); WS 4¾–5' (1.45–1.5 m)

Weight: M 2½–3 lb. (1.1–1.4 kg); F 3–3½ lb. (1.4–1.6 kg)

Male: Three color morphs. **Light morph** has a rusty red (rufous) back, light brown head and gray cheeks. White chin, breast, belly. Rusty flanks and upper legs. Long narrow wings, dark-tipped white primaries, white underside of wings and light rufous wing linings. Tail is white below, rufous above. Feathered legs. Large yellow feet. Yellow lips. Yellow-to-red eyes. **Rufous morph** is overall rufous with white wing linings. **Dark morph** is dark brown overall with rusty highlights; white trailing half of wings, seen in flight.

Female: same as male, noticeably larger

Juvenile: brown head, nape and wings, with a white chin, chest and belly, usually lacking any rufous, pale yellow eyes, thick dark line through each eye

Habitat: prairie, open land, agricultural areas, fields

Food: ground squirrels, prairie dogs, jackrabbits, other small to medium animals, snakes, insects, birds

Sounds: usually silent; when disturbed at the nest, gives a very weak, high-pitched whistle

Compare: Red-tailed Hawk (pg. 153) is smaller and lacks the rusty flanks and legs of the Ferruginous. The Swainson's Hawk (pg. 141) is smaller and has a distinctive two-toned underwing pattern and brown breast.

adult light

adult light dorsal

juvenile light

light morph

juvenile light

adult rufous

adult dark

juvenile dark

adult rufous

juvenile dark

Flight: long broad wings, wider near the base, with pointed wing tips and long "fingertips" (primaries); tail is short and broad; shallow wing beats alternate with short gliding; soars on thermals

Migration: complete to partial migrator, to western Texas, western Oklahoma and Mexico; some are non-migrators

Nesting: massive platform, low in a tree, occasionally on the ground; female and male build a new nest each year or repair an old nest, bringing in new nesting material; 1 brood

Eggs/Incubation: 2–4 bluish or white eggs, sometimes with brown markings; female incubates 28–33 days; male does the most hunting and feeds the nesting female before and after the young hatch

Fledging: 44–48 days; female feeds the young; male does the majority of hunting and brings food to the female, who feeds the chicks; upon leaving the nest (fledging), young continue to beg for their food; chicks learn how to hunt by watching and copying the behavior of their parents and are hunting by the end of the first summer

Stan's Notes: A bird of three color morphs—light, rufous and dark. Light is the most common; dark is rare. The Ferruginous rufous and dark morphs are often confused with the Harlan's subspecies of Red-tailed Hawk (pg. 153).

The largest open land hawk, or buteo. A hawk of the prairies. Perches on trees and fence posts to hunt. Usually hunts small to midsize animals such as ground squirrels and jackrabbits. Often stands and feeds on the ground.

A powerful hunter and regal bird, as the species name *regalis* implies. The common name "Ferruginous" means "ironlike" and refers to the rufous plumage on its flanks and legs.

Pairs perform courtship displays in the air, holding their wings above their backs while soaring (parachuting). Suddenly the male will dive at the female. When they meet, both grab each other in midair with their powerful feet.

Constructs a large nest in one of the few available trees in open prairie country. Returns to the same nest year after year. High rate of nest abandonment when nests are disturbed during the nesting season.

Golden Eagle

Aquila chrysaetos

YEAR-ROUND
WINTER

Family: Hawks, Eagles and Kites (Accipitridae)

Size: M 30–35" (76–88 cm); WS 6–6¾' (1.8–2.06 m)
F 34–37" (86–94 cm); WS 6¾–7¾' (2.06–2.36 m)

Weight: M 8–10 lb. (3.6–4.5 kg.); F 10–12 lb. (4.5–5.4 kg)

Male: A uniform dark brown body with a golden head and nape of neck. Gray bill with a dark tip and yellow around the base (cere). Brown leading half with gray trailing half of underwings, dark wing tips (primaries). Narrow gray tail bands with a wide dark terminal band. Yellow feet.

Female: similar to male, noticeably larger, with a wide, irregular gray band across the center of tail

Juvenile: white wrist patches and base of tail, nape is golden at all ages, long tail and wing feathers

Habitat: mountainous terrain, cliffs, valleys

Food: small to medium-large mammals, large birds, reptiles, large insects, carrion

Sounds: fairly quiet; can be vocal when one mate makes a kill and the other wants it; gives a high-pitched "yee-yee-yee" call; juveniles beg for food with a loud stuttering call

Compare: Similar size as Bald Eagle (pg. 165), but Golden Eagle lacks a white head and tail. Juvenile Golden, a large dark bird with consistent white markings on its wrists and base of tail, is often confused with juvenile Bald Eagle, which has inconsistent white marks all over its body and wings. Osprey (pg. 169) has a white body and dark wrist marks. Turkey Vulture (pg. 177) is smaller, with two-toned wings and a shorter tail.

adult

juvenile

juvenile

Flight: slow, strong, shallow wing beats interspersed with long periods of gliding; holds wings flat (horizontally) to a slightly upturned angle (dihedral) while soaring

Migration: complete to non-migrator, moving around to find food; individuals in the forested northern range in Alaska move and join those in other western states; most south of Canada do not migrate but will move in search of a plentiful food supply

Nesting: massive platform, on a ledge of a cliff face, sometimes in a tree; female and male build, bringing in large branches and other new nesting material each season, increasing the size over the years; 1 brood

Eggs/Incubation: 1–2 white eggs with brown markings; female and male incubate 43–45 days; male does the most hunting and feeds the nesting female before and after the young hatch

Fledging: 63–75 days; female and male feed young; male does the majority of hunting and brings food to the female, who feeds the chicks; upon leaving the nest (fledging), the young continue to beg for food, following parents around after they capture prey; chicks learn to hunt by watching and copying parental behavior

Stan's Notes: Large and powerful raptor that has no trouble taking larger prey such as jackrabbits, foxes, squirrels, rabbits, young deer and marmots. Hunts by perching or soaring and watching for movement. Inhabits mountainous terrain and open prairies, requiring large territories to provide ample food. Scavenges stillbirths and animals that died from winter kill.

Thought to mate for life, with pairs remaining together year-round, even migrating together. Renews its pair bond during late winter with spectacular high-flying courtship displays.

Usually nests on cliff faces. Uses a well-established nest that has been used for generations. Not uncommon for it to add things to the nest such as antlers, bones or barbed wire. A new nest is just a smattering of sticks, but as materials are added over the years, the nest can grow as high as 6 feet (1.8 m) tall.

Usually lays 2 eggs, with up to 3–4 days in between eggs. Young couples lay only 1 egg. Young eagles become independent of their parents by fall migration. The young take 6 years to obtain adult plumage, the same time that they start to breed.

Bald Eagle

Haliaeetus leucocephalus

YEAR-ROUND
MIGRATION
WINTER

Family: Hawks, Eagles and Kites (Accipitridae)

Size: M 31–35" (79–88 cm); WS 6–6¾' (1.8–2.06 m)
F 35–37" (88–94 cm); WS 6¾–8' (2.06–2.4 m)

Weight: M 8–10 lb. (3.6–4.5 kg); F 10–12 lb. (4.5–5.4 kg)

Male: Dark brown body and wings with a white head and tail. Large, curving yellow bill. Yellow feet. Long broad wings with well-defined individual primary feathers at the tip of wings.

Female: same as male, noticeably larger

Juvenile: first year has a very dark head, bill, body, wings, white wing linings; second through fourth years have a brown head covered with white speckles, body and wings spotted with white, dark-tipped gray bill, long tail and wings, appearing larger than adults; white head and tail at 4–6 years

Habitat: lakes, rivers, reservoirs, most large permanent water sources

Food: fish, carrion, birds (mainly ducks)

Sounds: very vocal in all seasons; gives a wide variety of calls, all short, shrill, high-pitched whistles, often ascending in pitch and repeated over and over

Compare: Golden Eagle (pg. 161) is similar in size, but it has a golden nape and lacks the white head and tail of the adult Bald Eagle. Juvenile Golden has consistent white marks on its wrists (carpals) and base of tail, with a black terminal tail band; juvenile Bald has inconsistent white marks over its body and wings. Osprey (pg. 169) has a white body and dark wrist marks. Turkey Vulture (pg. 177) has two-toned wings and a shorter tail.

adult

juvenile
4–6 years

juvenile
2–4 years

juvenile
1 year | fishing

Flight: long broad wings tipped with well-defined individual primary feathers; slow, shallow wing beats; holds wings flat (horizontally) while soaring

Migration: complete to non-migrator, moving around to find food during winter; northern birds move south to join resident birds; many do not migrate

Nesting: massive platform, usually in a tree; female and male build, bringing in new nesting material each season; 1 brood

Eggs/Incubation: 2–3 off-white eggs; female and male incubate 34–36 days; male does the most hunting and feeds the nesting female before and after the young hatch

Fledging: 75–90 days; female and male feed young; male does the majority of hunting and brings food to the female, who feeds the chicks; upon leaving the nest (fledging), young still beg for food, chasing parents around after they capture prey; chicks learn to hunt by watching the behavior of their parents

Stan's Notes: Driven to near extinction due to DDT poisoning and illegal killing. Now doing well across North America, especially in the South.

Like other raptors, eagles have 10 primary flight feathers, with 17 secondary flight feathers—4 more than other raptors. Adults acquire adult plumage at 4–6 years. Some retain their juvenile head plumage until 8 years. Younger juveniles have longer tail and wing feathers, up to 2 inches (5 cm), making them look larger than adults. Sometimes Bald juveniles are confused with Golden Eagles (pg. 161) due to their similar color and size.

In the midair mating ritual, one eagle will flip upside down and lock talons with another. Both tumble, then break apart to continue flight. Thought to mate for life but will switch mates if not successful reproducing or if one mate dies. Returns to the same nest each year, adding more sticks, enlarging it to massive proportions, at times up to 1,000 pounds (450 kg).

Eagles in southern latitudes are much smaller than those in northern latitudes. Florida eagles are the smallest, while Alaskan eagles are particularly large. Southern females are smaller than northern males. Southern eagles can be up to 7 inches (18 cm) smaller than northern eagles of the same sex.

Osprey

Pandion haliaetus

YEAR-ROUND
MIGRATION
SUMMER
WINTER

Family: Osprey (Pandionidae)

Size: L 21–24" (53–61 cm); WS 5–5½' (1.5–1.7 m)

Weight: 2⅛–4⅛ lb. (1–1.9 kg)

Male: Large eagle-like raptor with a white breast and belly and nearly black back. Dark bill. White head, sometimes with a dark forehead. Dark line through the eyes (auricular), extending to the back of head. Pale yellow eyes. Long wings with black wrist (carpal) patches and tips of the primaries. White body and axillaries. Two-toned wings, white leading, dark trailing. Gray feet.

Female: similar to male, slightly larger, often has a necklace of brown streaks on the breast; necklace is unreliable for female identification

Juvenile: similar to adults, with a tan-to-rust breast and wing linings, orange eyes (Jun–Jan); appears like an adult by 1 year of age

Habitat: lakes, rivers, reservoirs, most large permanent water sources

Food: primarily live fish; sometimes will eat dead fish, reptiles, amphibians and small waterfowl

Sounds: very vocal in all seasons; gives a wide variety of calls, each a short high-pitched shrill or whistle, often ascending in pitch, repeated over and over

Compare: Bald Eagle (pg. 165) has an all-white head and tail and a large yellow bill. Juvenile Bald Eagle is brown with white speckles, lacking a white body. Look for a white belly, dark eye stripe and black carpal patches to identify the Osprey.

juvenile

juvenile

adult fishing

Flight: long narrow wings, cupped or bowed downward and angled (crooked) backward, often appearing swept back or in an M shape when in flight; fast, shallow wing beats; hovers before diving

Migration: complete migrator, to the Gulf Coast, Mexico, Central and South America, migrating alone during the day; non-migrator in Florida and much of the Gulf Coast

Nesting: platform, often in a tall tree, on a man-made tower equipped with a wooden platform, on a large light post, bridge, buoy or other human structure; female and male construct, bringing in new nesting material each season; 1 brood

Eggs/Incubation: 2–4 white eggs with brown marks; female and male incubate 32–42 days; male does the most hunting and feeds the nesting female before and after the young hatch

Fledging: 48–58 days; male and female feed young; male does the majority of hunting and brings fish to the female, who feeds the chicks; upon leaving the nest (fledging), the young continue to beg for food, chasing parents after they catch a fish; chicks learn to fish by watching and copying parental behavior

Stan's Notes: The only species in its family. Neither a hawk nor an eagle, it has unique feet, with two toes that face forward and two backward, unlike the feet of hawks and eagles, which have three forward and one backward. It is also the only raptor that plunges into water feet first, often completely submerging to catch fish. Hunts from heights of up to 100 feet (30 m). Often hovers for a few seconds before diving. Can take off from the water's surface while carrying fish. Carries a fish in a head-first position for better aerodynamics. Often forced by Bald Eagles (pg. 165) to drop its catch, which eagles snatch and eat.

Also known as Fish Hawk, feeding mostly on live fish. Nearly always seen in association with water. Some Ospreys are comfortable having people around their nests. Others are shy. Most don't try to nest until they are at least 3 years old. Young return to the nest each night after fledging, unlike other raptors.

Can live up to 20–25 years. Recent studies show Ospreys mate perhaps for life or until one dies, after which the survivor takes a new mate. Courtship includes high circling and vocalizations by both members, with the male hovering in flight. Mated pairs do not migrate together or go to the same wintering grounds.

YEAR-ROUND

Black Vulture
Coragyps atratus

Family: Vultures (Cathartidae)

Size: L 25–28" (64–71 cm); WS 4½–5¼' (1.4–1.6 m)

Weight: 4–5 lb. (1.8–2.3 kg)

Male: All-black bird with a dark gray wrinkled head and gray legs. Short square tail. During flight, all-black body and wings, with light gray wing tips (primaries). Long broad wings with well-defined primary feathers.

Female: same as male

Juvenile: similar to adults, with unwrinkled black skin on the head

Habitat: open country, farm fields, woodlands, along highways, close to rivers, lakes, creeks and other permanent water sources

Food: carrion, just about any dead animal of any size, occasionally capturing small live mammals and birds; also known to eat vegetables and plants; parents regurgitate for young

Sounds: mostly mute; hisses, grunts and groans

Compare: Slightly smaller than the Turkey Vulture (pg. 177) and lacking the bright red head. Turkey Vulture has two-toned wings, a black leading edge and light gray trailing edge. Black Vulture has shorter gray-tipped wings and a shorter tail than the Turkey Vulture. Adult and juvenile Bald Eagles (pg. 165) are larger and lack the two-toned wings of Black Vulture.

juvenile

juvenile

Flight: short, wide black wings with gray tips (primaries), holding wings at a slight upsweep and also flat; fast, flicking wing beats followed by gliding; teeters back and forth in air currents during flight

Migration: non-migrator; moves around all year to find food

Nesting: no nest, or minimal nest on the ground under thick vegetation, in a protected cliff, cave or broken-off tree trunk, on the first floor of an abandoned building; 1 brood

Eggs/Incubation: 1–3 light green eggs with dark markings; female and male incubate 37–45 days; male forages much more than the female and feeds her before and after the young hatch

Fledging: 75–80 days; female and male feed young; nestlings and fledglings are fed regurgitated food by both parents; upon leaving the nest (fledging), young follow their parents, hissing and grunting for food; chicks watch the parents and learn to forage for food; young remain with adults until the first winter

Stan's Notes: Also called Black Buzzard. The only member of its genus, *Coragyps*. Holds its wings straight out to the sides with wing tips curved up during flight. This is unlike Turkey Vulture (pg. 177), which holds its wings in a slight V shape.

Prefers fresh carrion, but also feeds on decaying meat. Seems to be less skilled at finding carrion, often following Turkey Vultures to find food. Sense of smell is believed to be less developed than in Turkey Vultures; some think the Black has no sense of smell. More aggressive than Turkey Vultures while feeding, with many fights and squabbles. When startled, regurgitates powerfully and accurately onto the intruder, especially while defending the nest.

More gregarious than Turkey Vulture, often nesting and roosting with other Black Vultures, especially after breeding season. Families stay together for up to a year. It is thought a male and female will mate for life. Often seen in groups at watering holes, drinking freely and bathing regularly. Pairs preen each other; some individuals preen other bird species.

Turkey Vulture

Cathartes aura

YEAR-ROUND
SUMMER

Family: Vultures (Cathartidae)

Size: L 26–32" (66–80 cm); WS 5½–6' (1.7–1.8 m)

Weight: 3–4 lb. (1.4–1.8 kg)

Male: Dark brown-to-black plumage. Naked red head. Wings look two-toned during flight, with dark underwing coverts and a gray trailing edge and tip. Wing tips (primaries) end in fingerlike projections. Long tail. Hooked ivory bill. Reddish legs and feet, usually stained with some tan to off-white.

Female: same as male, slightly smaller

Juvenile: similar to adults, with a gray-to-black head and bill

Habitat: open country, farm fields, woodlands, along highways, close to rivers, lakes, creeks and other permanent water sources

Food: carrion, just about any dead animal of any size; parents regurgitate for young

Sounds: mostly mute; hisses, grunts and groans; young grunt to beg for food

Compare: Black Vulture (pg. 173) has shorter wings and a short square tail. Adult and juvenile Bald Eagles (pg. 165) are larger and lack Turkey Vulture's two-toned wings. Unlike the Black Vulture and Bald Eagle, Turkey Vulture holds its wings in a shallow V shape during flight and tilts back and forth from wing tip to wing tip. Look for the two-toned wings while the Turkey Vulture is soaring to help identify.

adult

adult drying

juvenile

Flight: two-toned wings show a black leading edge and light gray trailing edge; holds wings in a shallow V shape and teeters back and forth in air currents during flight

Migration: complete to non-migrator, to southern states, Mexico, Central and South America

Nesting: no nest, or minimal nest on a cliff, in a cave or broken-off tree trunk; 1 brood

Eggs/Incubation: 1–3 white eggs with brown markings; female and male incubate 38–41 days; male forages much than the female and feeds her before and after the young hatch

Fledging: 66–88 days; female and male feed young; male does the majority of foraging and brings food to the female, who feeds the chicks; upon leaving the nest (fledging), the young still beg for food, chasing their parents after they find food; chicks learn to forage by watching and copying their parents; young remain with adults until the first winter

Stan's Notes: One of the few birds with a developed sense of smell, which it uses to locate carrion. Usually prefers freshly dead, but it will take rotting carcasses. The naked head reduces the risk of feather fouling, a result from sticking its head into a carcass cavity. The vulture has a strong bill for tearing apart flesh, but unlike hawks and eagles, it has weak feet that are more suited to walking than grasping and killing. Recent studies show this bird is closely related to storks, not birds of prey.

Gregarious, roosting in large groups. At night, lowers its body temperature as much as 10 degrees. Perches in trees with wings outstretched, sunning itself first thing in the morning to warm up. Also suns itself to dry its feathers after rain and rid its body of ticks or mites. Can't sweat to keep cool. Instead, defecates on its legs to achieve evaporative cooling (urohydrosis). Will vomit stomach contents on a trespasser if disturbed at the nest site.

Called "Turkey" for its bald head and dark feathers, resembling a Wild Turkey. "Vulture," from the Latin word *vulturus* (tearer), refers to how it removes flesh to eat. Brings food to its young in its stomach (crop) and regurgitates. Lack of a voice box (syrinx) limits it to hissing, grunting and groaning. This bird has few natural predators.

SUMMER

Elf Owl

Micrathene whitneyi

OWLS

Family: Owls (Strigidae)

Size: L 5–6" (13–15 cm); WS 12–14" (30–36 cm)

Weight: 1¼–1½ oz. (35–43 g)

Male: A tiny non-eared owl with a large rounded head and sparrow-sized body. Overall gray with tan and white spots. Cinnamon buff facial disk and a faint dark outline. Bright yellow eyes. White lines above eyes (superciliary). Small greenish yellow bill. Short tail.

Female: same as male, slightly more rufous

Juvenile: light gray with a dark mask around the eyes

Habitat: scrublands, deserts, open woodlands, parks

Food: large insects, crickets, beetles, spiders, small reptiles such as lizards and snakes

Sounds: loud, raspy barklike series of calls with a steady rhythm; strings a series of 6–8 notes together, with middle notes louder

Compare: Smaller than Western Screech-Owl (pg. 197), which has ear tufts and a whiter face. Flammulated Owl (pg. 189) is slightly larger, has ear tufts and dark eyes.

adult

chicks

Flight: very broad, short wings with round tips; usually short undulating flights with rapid, fluttering wing beats; buoyant flight much like a moth; may hover at the nest cavity or right before landing

Migration: complete migrator, to southern Mexico and Central America

Nesting: cavity, former woodpecker hole in a saguaro cactus or tree, only few will use a man-made nest box; does not add any nesting material; 1 brood

Eggs/Incubation: 2–4 white eggs; female incubates 23–25 days; male does the most hunting and feeds the nesting female before and after the young hatch

Fledging: 28–33 days; female feeds young when they are very young; male does the majority of hunting and brings food to the female, who usually feeds the chicks; when the young are older, food is dropped into the nest cavity and the chicks feed themselves; upon leaving the nest (fledging), the young still beg for food, following their parents around; chicks learn to hunt by watching and copying the behavior of the parents

Stan's Notes: The smallest owl in the United States and the world. A migratory owl, arriving in southern parts of Texas in late March. It has adapted well to human encroachment, often nesting in parks and yards. Males arrive first and claim a territory and nest cavity. When the females arrive in 1–2 weeks, males call them to their cavities. A male's call can be quite loud and heard several hundred feet away. Once a female is attracted, the male courts her, feeding her insects. Female roosts in the cavity for up to several weeks before laying eggs.

Has an unusual butterfly or mothlike flight, often hovering at the nest cavity for a few seconds before landing. Hunts from a low perch during the night, searching for large insects, spiders and small reptiles on the desert floor. Sometimes runs on the ground after its prey. Removes wings from moths and stingers from scorpions before eating. Will hang from flowers, waiting for a visit from nocturnal pollinating insects.

YEAR-ROUND

Ferruginous Pygmy-Owl
Glaucidium brasilianum

OWLS

Family: Owls (Strigidae)

Size: L 6–7" (15–18 cm); WS 12–15" (30–38 cm)

Weight: 2¼–2½ oz. (64–71 g)

Male: Small non-eared owl. Overall rusty brown with a streaked cap, yellow eyes and white eyebrows. Blotchy back and upper surface of wings. Large vertical brown streaks on chest, extending into the belly. Two large dark marks on nape of neck, looking like eyes on the back of head. Greenish bill, yellow-tipped. Long narrow tail with many dark bands.

Female: same as male

Juvenile: darker version of the adults

Habitat: wide variety including riparian areas, mesquite thickets, dense woodlands, cottonwood groves, deserts, plantations

Food: large insects, small animals, small birds, reptiles

Sounds: series of rapid single-whistle notes, with 3 notes per second, repeated about 50–60 times

Compare: Slightly larger than Elf Owl (pg. 181), which lacks large vertical brown streaks on its breast. The Ferruginous has a longer tail than Elf Owl, with many dark tail bands. Western Screech-Owl (pg. 197) is slightly larger, with ear tufts.

adult

adults

Flight: short wide wings with round tips; usually short direct flights with rapid wing beats

Migration: non-migrator; moves around to find food and a roosting cavity

Nesting: cavity, natural tree cavity, former woodpecker hole or man-made cavity such as a wooden nest box; does not add any nesting material; 1 brood

Eggs/Incubation: 3–5 white eggs; female incubates 26–28 days; male does the most hunting and feeds the nesting female before and after the young hatch

Fledging: 27–30 days; female feeds the young when they are very young; male does the most hunting and brings food to the female, who feeds the chicks; when the young are older, food is dropped into the nest cavity and the chicks feed themselves; upon leaving the nest (fledging), the young continue to beg for food, following the parents around; chicks learn to hunt by watching and copying the behavior of the parents, remaining with their parents until the following winter, when the adults prepare for nesting once again

Stan's Notes: A very tiny, uncommon owl, a bit larger than a sparrow. Very common in Mexico along the Pacific Coast, but in the United States it is found only in the southern tip of Texas and south central Arizona. Usually in lowlands and foothills, often in wetlands (riparian) areas, but it can occur in mesquite thickets and saguaro deserts. Fairly tolerant of people. Does well in plantations and other disturbed habitats. Some can be seen in suburban parks and yards.

A daytime (diurnal) hunter, frequently active at dawn and dusk (crepuscular). Hunts from a perch, quickly flying down to catch prey, which can range in size from a small insect to a bird larger than itself. Often flicks its long narrow tail up and down when perched.

Monogamous, with a long-term pair bond. Owlets hatch at different times (asynchronously), resulting in size differences between the oldest and youngest. The young compete for food, often fighting for it and suffering some injuries in the process.

gray morph

Flammulated Owl

Otus flammeolus

Family: Owls (Strigidae)

Size: L 6–7" (15–18 cm); WS 13–16" (33–40 cm)

Weight: 1¾–2 oz. (50–57 g)

Male: Small eared owl, occurring in two color morphs. Squared head, with an incomplete outline consisting of a narrow black line around the facial disk. Short, rounded ear tufts, which can lay flat and be invisible. Dark eyes, a small greenish bill and very short tail. When perching, wing tips project slightly past the tip of tail. **Gray morph** is slate gray with wavy streaks of white and black. **Red morph** is rusty red with streaks of white, black and red.

Female: same as male, slightly larger

Juvenile: overall gray with dark eyes and a dark outline around the facial disk, lacks ear tufts

Habitat: coniferous forests with Douglas Fir or Ponderosa Pine, dense woodlands with grassy openings

Food: insects, spiders, centipedes, scorpions

Sounds: low, soft, slow raspy hoot repeated every second or every other second, sometimes alternating with a 2-note hoot

Compare: Smaller and thinner than the Western Screech-Owl (pg. 197), which has yellow eyes, shorter ears, a dark bill, longer wings and is overall gray. Flammulated Owl is the only small owl with ear tufts and dark eyes.

adult gray

adult gray

juvenile gray

red morph

Flight: long broad wings with round tips; usually short direct flights with slow, full wing beats; buoyant flight, fluttering silently to a branch

Migration: complete migrator, to Mexico and Central America

Nesting: cavity, natural tree cavity, old woodpecker hole or man-made cavity; does not add any nesting material; 1 brood

Eggs/Incubation: 3–4 white eggs, female incubates 25–26 days; male does the most hunting and feeds the nesting female

Fledging: 26–27 days; female feeds young when they are very young; male does the most hunting and brings food to the female, who usually feeds the chicks; when the young are older, food is dropped into the nest cavity and the chicks feed themselves; upon fledging, the young still beg, following the parents around for food; chicks learn to hunt by watching their parents

Stan's Notes: One of the smallest owls in the United States and also in the world. A nearly exclusive insect and arthropod eater. Feeds in flight by catching flying insects, such as moths, but also takes insects on the ground by perching and watching, then flying down to grab them.

The only small owl with dark eyes and ear tufts. Two color morphs, with the red slightly more common in thicker forests and the gray in woods with less cover. Found in pine or oak forests.

Highly migratory, with long broad wings that are well suited for long migratory flights. Migrates at night to southern Mexico and Central America. Closely related to Western Screech-Owl (pg. 197), but the screech-owl doesn't migrate.

Often returns to the same area to nest, presumably with the same mate. Several nests may be found fairly close together, suggesting semi-colonial nesting.

A unique hoarse, low-frequency call produced by a specialized throat structure. It's often difficult to pinpoint where the call is coming from due to its low frequency and volume. Often repeats the call for many hours at night early during breeding season. Falls silent later in the season.

Northern Saw-whet Owl

Aegolius acadicus

OWLS

YEAR-ROUND
WINTER

Family: Owls (Strigidae)

Size: L 7–8" (18–20 cm); WS 17–20" (43–50 cm)

Weight: 2–3 oz. (57–85 g)

Male: Small tawny brown owl. Head is large compared with its body. Large, obvious facial disk. White eyebrows, yellow eyes and small dark bill. Wide, vertical, rusty brown streaking on a white breast and belly. Distinctive light markings on the back and wings. Short tail.

Female: same as male, slightly larger

Juvenile: dark brown with a unique rusty brown belly

Habitat: mixed coniferous and deciduous forests, dense woodlands, wooded backyards

Food: mice, small birds, insects

Sounds: repeats a one-note "too" whistle, sounding like "too-too-too-too" and lasting for several minutes to up to an hour; also repeats a "sch-whet" call reminiscent of a saw blade being sharpened, but this call is rarely heard

Compare: Much smaller than Barred Owl (pg. 221), which has dark eyes. The Great Horned Owl (pg. 225) is much larger and has large, obvious ear tufts. The Short-eared Owl (pg. 213) is twice as large as the Saw-whet.

adult

juvenile

standing on prey

Flight: very wide and relatively long wings for such a small raptor; buoyant flight with fluttering wing beats; flies silently

Migration: partial to non-migrator; moves around in winter to find food

Nesting: cavity, former woodpecker cavity, wooden nest box; does not add any nesting material; 1 brood

Eggs/Incubation: 5–6 white eggs; female and male incubate 26–28 days; male does the most hunting and feeds the nesting female before and after the young hatch

Fledging: 27–34 days; male and female feed young; male does the majority of hunting and brings food to the female, who feeds the chicks; upon leaving the nest (fledging), the young continue to beg for food, following parents around after they capture prey; chicks learn to hunt by watching and copying the behavior of their parents

Stan's Notes: Our smallest owl but not often recognized as an owl because of its diminutive size. The common name "Saw-whet" was given for its raspy whistling call, which sounds like a saw blade being sharpened.

A resident throughout most northern states. Will move out of some regions and into others during winter. Usually found in mixed forests, roosting in cavities, conifers or thick vegetation. Can be tame and approachable, especially during winter, when it often roosts in thick coniferous hedges.

Well-developed fringe and down pile on primary flight feathers result in silent flight. Strictly a nighttime hunter. Eats mainly mice, regardless of the time of year. Will often catch a mouse during the night, return to its daytime roost and stand on its prey until the following evening before dining.

Young hatch asynchronously. The youngest often perishes when the older owlets fledge, leaving it behind without parental care. Known to nest in Wood Duck boxes put up by landowners.

gray morph

Western Screech-Owl

Megascops kennicottii

Family: Owls (Strigidae)

Size: L 8–9" (20–23 cm); WS 19–23" (48–58 cm)

Weight: 5–5½ oz. (142–156 g)

Male: Small eared owl that has two color morphs (dichromatic). Both morphs have a short tail, bright yellow eyes, a small dark bill and short ear tufts that can lay flat, becoming invisible. **Gray morph** has black and white highlights, with dark streaks running along the sides of face, extending to the chest. **Brown morph** is mainly tawny with black and white highlights and a dark outline around the facial disk.

Female: same as male, slightly larger

Juvenile: light gray, usually with smaller ear tufts or none

Habitat: wide variety including deciduous forests, parks, desert scrub, riparian areas, wooded canyons, wooded suburban backyards and orchards

Food: large insects, reptiles, small animals, songbirds

Sounds: short series of single-note calls given in a trill; female is slightly higher in pitch than the male

Compare: One of three screech-owls with ear tufts. Eastern Screech-Owl (pg. 201) has a similar size, but less barring and a greenish bill. To distinguish a Western Screech-Owl from an Eastern, compare their very different ranges and their calls. Flammulated Owl (pg. 189) is smaller, with dark eyes and a thinner, less robust body.

adult
gray

juvenile
gray

brown morph

Flight: long broad wings with round tips; usually short flights with fluttering wing beats; buoyant flight, fluttering silently to a branch

Migration: non-migrator; moves around to find food and a roosting cavity during winter

Nesting: cavity, natural tree cavity, old woodpecker hole or man-made cavity; does not add any nesting material; 1 brood

Eggs/Incubation: 2-6 white eggs; female incubates 21–30 days; male does the most hunting and feeds the nesting female before and after the young hatch

Fledging: 25–30 days; female feeds the very young; male hunts the most and brings food to the female, who usually feeds the chicks; male may occasionally feed the chicks before they reach 2 weeks of age; older chicks feed on food dropped into the nest; upon fledging, the young follow their parents around and beg for food; chicks learn to hunt by copying the behavior of their parents, remaining with them until the end of summer

Stan's Notes: Once considered a subspecies of the Eastern Screech-Owl (pg. 201). Most are gray; others are mainly brown. In Texas they are very light gray. The farther north and west in the range, the darker the plumage.

Nocturnal, becoming active shortly after dusk. Hunts during the first few hours of darkness in close proximity to the nest. Perches on branches about 5 feet (1.5 m) above the ground in search of prey. Caches extra food in cavities to consume later.

Needs trees at least a foot in diameter for nesting and roosting, so usually found in areas with old growth. A secondary cavity nester, nesting in tree cavities made by other birds. Roosts in cavities or thick vegetation during the day. Will often look out of the cavity during the day, sunning itself. Densities are around 1 bird per square mile (2–3 birds per sq. km).

Monogamous, with a long-term pair bond. Adults may attack an intruder near the nest or perform a distraction display to draw the trespasser away. Stays near the nest cavity all year. Reuses the same cavity, sometimes for many decades.

gray morph

Eastern Screech-Owl

Megascops asio

YEAR-ROUND

Family: Owls (Strigidae)

Size: L 8–10" (20–25 cm); WS 18–24" (45–61 cm)

Weight: 5–6 oz. (142–170 g)

Male: A small eared owl, with two permanent color morphs (dichromatic). Both morphs have dark vertical streaking on the breast and belly and a black line outlining the facial disk. Bright yellow eyes. Greenish bill. Small tufts of feathers on the head, becoming invisible when flattened back on the head. **Gray morph** is a mottled gray and white. **Red morph** is brown (rust) with white.

Female: same as male, slightly larger

Juvenile: lighter color than the same morph adult, usually smaller ear tufts

Habitat: forests, dense woodlands, wooded backyards, parks

Food: large insects, mice and other small mammals, songbirds, small snakes

Sounds: tremulous, descending whiny trill that lasts a long time; can be very quiet and difficult to hear even when near; seldom gives a screeching call; female is slightly higher in pitch than the male

Compare: Northern Saw-whet Owl (pg. 193) lacks ear tufts, has a whiter face and thick, vertical brown streaks on its breast and belly. The Western Screech-Owl (pg. 197) is less common and has more barring on its breast.

adult gray

juvenile gray

red morph

Flight: long broad wings with round tips; usually short direct flights with rapid, full wing beats; buoyant flight, fluttering silently to a branch

Migration: non-migrator; moves around to find food and a roosting cavity

Nesting: cavity, natural tree cavity, former woodpecker hole or man-made cavity such as a wooden nest box; does not add any nesting material; 1 brood

Eggs/Incubation: 4–5 white eggs; female incubates 25–26 days; male does the most hunting and feeds the nesting female before and after the young hatch

Fledging: 26–27 days; female feeds young when they are very young; male does the most hunting and brings food to the female, who usually feeds the chicks; male may occasionally feed the chicks himself before they reach 2 weeks of age; when the young are older, food is dropped into the nest cavity and the chicks feed themselves; upon leaving the nest (fledging), the young continue to beg for food, following parents around; chicks learn to hunt by watching and copying the behavior of the parents, remaining with their parents until the following winter, which is when the adults prepare for nesting once again

Stan's Notes: A small and very common owl in the South. Gray morph is more common than the red. Excellent hearing and eyesight. Active only after dark. During winter, often seen sunning itself at a nest box hole (former Wood Duck house). While the male and female don't roost together in winter, they roost nearby and interact with each other. Thought to mate for life but will take another mate after the death of a partner. Prefers to nest in the same nest box or cavity from year to year. Even though the eggs are laid days apart, they still hatch within a span of 24–48 hours.

This owl has the most diverse diet of all of the U.S. owls. Video studies by this author of nesting and roosting Eastern Screech-Owls over a 4-year period revealed that 100 percent of the food intake in winter consisted of small mammals and songbirds such as American Goldfinches and Black-capped Chickadees. During spring and summer the diet was mainly June bugs, other large insects and small mammals such as mice.

Western

Burrowing Owl

Athene cunicularia

YEAR-ROUND
SUMMER
WINTER

Family: Owls (Strigidae)

Size: L 9–10" (23–25 cm); WS 20–24" (50–61 cm)

Weight: 4½–5 oz. (128–142 g)

Male: A small brown owl with very long, nearly bare legs. Back covered with white spots. White belly with many brown horizontal bars. Bright white eyebrows and throat. Yellow eyes with a gray or yellow bill. Short tail.

Female: same as male, slightly smaller

Juvenile: same as adults, with a brown belly, lacking the spots and barring

Habitat: fields, open backyards, golf courses, airports, along dirt roads

Food: insects, small mammals, lizards, small birds

Sounds: vocal during breeding season; male gives a call of 4–6 hoots that sounds like "hoo-hoo-hoo-hoooo"; also barks, hisses and repeats wheezy, raspy calls; female voice is higher than that of the male

Compare: Short-eared Owl (pg. 213) is much larger and lacks the white throat and long legs. Burrowing is much smaller than Great Horned Owl (pg. 225) and lacks the feather tuft "horns." Spends most of its time on the ground, compared with the tree-loving Great Horns. The Eastern Screech-Owl (pg. 201) has ear tufts and lacks the long legs of Burrowing Owl. The Barred Owl (pg. 221) is larger and has dark eyes.

adult
Western

juvenile
Western

juveniles at burrow

Florida

Flight: long broad wings; fast, fluttery wing beats with direct flight to and from the burrow; rarely seen in flight

Migration: partial to non-migrator in Texas and western Oklahoma, non-migrator in Florida; moves around to find food during winter

Nesting: cavity, old underground mammal den, occasionally widens it by kicking dirt back, sometimes digs its own burrow, many choose nest sites along roads, takes well to an artificial (man-made) burrow made of PVC pipe or drain tile leading to a small underground chamber; adds some nesting material such as cow pies, horse dung, grass and feathers; 1 brood

Eggs/Incubation: 6–11 white eggs; female incubates 26–30 days; male hunts the most and brings food to the sitting female

Fledging: 25–28 days; female and male feed young; male does the majority of hunting and takes food to the female, who feeds the chicks; upon leaving the nest (fledging), the young continue to beg for food, waiting at the burrow for the adults to bring food; chicks learn to hunt by watching and copying the behavior of their parents, staying with them until migration

Stan's Notes: This is a very small, uncommon owl of fields, rural roads and airports. An owl that will hunt during the day, perching on the ground, on short posts or in trees. Often seen standing or sleeping around the den entrance in the daytime, with young remaining around the burrow during the day.

Unlike all other owl species in North America, the Burrowing male is larger than the female. Legs and feet are not protected with heavy feathering, but this is not needed for safely catching its main diet, insects. Will bob its head while doing deep knee bends if agitated or threatened. Seems to tolerate people well.

Nests in small family units or small colonies; in Florida it is frequently in family units. Male will often move the family to a new den when the young are a few weeks old, usually because of excessive insect infestation in the burrow.

Main population in western states and the Florida population are not doing well. Declining in nearly all locations.

Long-eared Owl

Asio otus

YEAR-ROUND
WINTER

Family: Owls (Strigidae)

Size: L 14–16" (36–40 cm); WS 30–36" (76–91 cm)

Weight: 8–9 oz. (227–255 g)

Male: Overall brown to gray, appearing tall and thin. Rusty red-to-orange face (facial disk) outlined with a thin black and white line. Dark vertical stripe through the eyes. Two thick, vertical white lines between the eyes. Long dark ear tufts, appearing close together. Heavy dark streaking on breast and belly. Large yellow eyes. Large feet and short legs.

Female: same as male, slightly larger, overall darker with more orange

Juvenile: similar to adults, light gray with a dark face

Habitat: thick coniferous forests, open fields, marshes, meadows

Food: small rodents and other small mammals, birds

Sounds: male repeats hoots every 3 seconds and female responds with a higher, softer call; also gives a barking call and a whining call; frequently silent when not breeding

Compare: Smaller and thinner than the Great Horned Owl (pg. 225), with ear tufts close together on top of head. Similar size as the Short-eared Owl (pg. 213), which lacks long ear tufts and a rusty face. Nearly twice the size of the Western Screech-Owl (pg. 197).

concealment posture

juvenile

adult

adult

Flight: long wings with a distinctive black wrist mark below and a bold tan patch above near the primaries; deep, slow wing beats; hunts by floating on air with wings outstretched before dropping to the ground; while soaring, occasionally swoops and claps wings together under the body; male courtship flight is zigzagged, sometimes with a loud wing clap that sounds like a wooden stick breaking

Migration: complete migrator, to northern parts of southern states; non-migrator in some locations

Nesting: platform, in a tree, rarely on the ground; takes over the nest of a Red-tailed Hawk (pg. 153), Great Blue Heron, American Crow or other bird; 1 brood

Eggs/Incubation: 4–6 white eggs; female incubates 26–28 days; male does the most hunting and feeds the nesting female before and after the young hatch

Fledging: 23–26 days; male and female feed young; male does the majority of hunting and brings food to the female, who feeds the chicks; upon leaving the nest (fledging), the young still beg for food, at first waiting for the parents to bring food, then following them around; chicks learn to hunt by watching their parents, staying with them until the end of summer

Stan's Notes: Thought to be the most slender of all large owls. Named "Long-eared" for the tufts of feathers that look like ears. Raises the tufts and constricts its body feathers to look thinner and taller, like a branch, when danger comes near. Known to sit straight up against a tree trunk for camouflage (concealment posture), but it will strike this pose only when a predator or mobbing birds are near.

Perhaps the most nocturnal of owls. Roosts close to a tree trunk during the day and doesn't leave until several hours after dark. May roost with other Long-eared Owls in winter. Often uses the same perch each night, with pellets accumulating below.

Both sexes perform wing claps during courtship. Monogamous, with a long-term pair bond. Some pairs stay together all winter. Sometimes found in a loose colony that consists of several pairs nesting in close proximity.

Hunts on the wing, using its eyesight at night, cruising over fields and marshes. Moves to various destinations when the local food supply dwindles due to weather changes. Studies of banded owls have shown that some Long-eared young travel over 1,500 miles (2,415 km) to find their own territory.

Short-eared Owl

Asio flammeus

YEAR-ROUND
WINTER

Family: Owls (Strigidae)

Size: L 14–17" (36–43 cm); WS 3–3¼' (.9–1 m)

Weight: 11–12 oz. (312–340 g)

Male: Overall brown-to-tan plumage. Heavy streaks on the breast, with a lighter belly and spotted back. Very short, tiny ear tufts, usually not noticeable. Long wide wings with a distinctive black wrist (carpal) mark beneath and prominent tan patch near the upper end (primaries), with black tips. Dark patches around bright yellow eyes. Large head and short neck.

Female: same as male, overall darker with a darker face

Juvenile: similar to adults, light tan with a dark face

Habitat: open fields, meadows, marshes, prairies

Food: small mammals, birds

Sounds: harsh hissing any time of year; calls a soft "poo-poo-poo" during breeding season; female call is more quiet than the male and juvenile call is hoarser; gives an alarm bark; claps wings during flight, sounding like a whip cracking

Compare: Larger than Burrowing Owl (pg. 205), which lacks ear tufts and has a white throat and long legs. Long-eared Owl (pg. 209) is about the same size, but it has long ear tufts and a rusty red face. Northern Harrier (pg. 121) has a similar flight pattern, but the males are all white underneath with black wing tips; female Harries are rust brown and lack the dark mask around the eyes.

adult

adult at nest

hunting

Flight: long wide wings; long, slow, stiff wing beats and erratic flight, distinctive and buoyant, like that of a butterfly; floats on air with wings outstretched, sometimes hovering above prey before dropping to the ground; occasionally swoops and claps wings together underneath the body while in flight, creating a whip-cracking sound

Migration: complete to non-migrator, moving out of northern regions in winter to southern states

Nesting: ground nest, well concealed in thick vegetation and made with a loose gathering of dried grass; 1 brood

Eggs/Incubation: 4–7 white eggs; female incubates 26–30 days; male does the most hunting and feeds the nesting female before and after the young hatch

Fledging: 23–36 days; male and female feed young; male does the majority of hunting, both parents bring food and feed the young; upon leaving the nest (fledging), the young continue to beg for food, at first waiting for the parents to bring food, then following them around to be fed; chicks learn to hunt by watching and copying the behavior of their parents

Stan's Notes: An owl of Alaska and northern Canada. Also found throughout northern states in the Lower 48. Often up to a dozen Shorties take up winter residency in large open areas and remain there all winter to hunt. Can be common in some years, nonexistent in others.

Main diet consists of small rodents such as voles and mice. Hunts over open fields, like Long-eared Owls (pg. 209), often floating on air just before dropping onto prey. Frequently starts to hunt 30 minutes to an hour before sunset. Hunts during the day when weather is overcast, making it one of the few owls you can see during the day. Look for the dark mask "mascara" around the eyes to help identify. Ear tufts are very short and hard to see unless the owl is perched and in alert posture.

Coughs up pellets in the same way as other owls. Owl pellets contain the undigested parts of prey such as bones and fur. Look for pellets below favorite perches.

Will perch on small trees out in the open to survey the area. Also sits on branches or fence posts to feed. At the nest, adults perform distraction displays to lure intruders away from the site. Sometimes nesting is semicolonial.

male

Barn Owl

Tyto alba

YEAR-ROUND
SUMMER

Family: Owls (Tytonidae)

Size: L 16–19" (40–48 cm); WS 3–3½' (.9–1.1 m)

Weight: 1–1¼ lb. (.5–.6 kg)

Male: A non-eared owl. Rusty tan on the back of head, back, wings and tail. Heart-shaped white facial disk, outlined in darker rusty brown. White breast and belly with many scattered tiny dark marks. Dark eyes. Long gray legs and gray feet. Ivory bill. White wing linings.

Female: slightly larger than male, with a rusty wash over a spotted breast and belly

Juvenile: fuzzy-looking with light gray-to-white plumage and a distinct heart-shaped face

Habitat: farm fields, woods, cliffs, semi-wooded areas, suburban areas, prairies

Food: mice and other small animals, birds, snakes

Sounds: harsh hissing any time of year; female call is more quiet than the male; juvenile call is hoarser

Compare: Easily identified by the white heart-shaped facial disk and dark eyes. The Snowy Owl (pg. 229) is much larger, has white plumage and lacks a heart-shaped face. Slightly larger than Short-eared Owl (pg. 213), which has a streaked chest and belly, dark marks around each eye and a less defined facial disk.

male hunting

female

juveniles

female

Flight: long broad wings, rounded at the tip and cupped or bowed downward during flight; slow, shallow wing beats with silent flight

Migration: non-migrator to partial; will congregate in groups during winter

Nesting: cavity, in a man-made structure such as a barn, other outbuilding or wooden nest box, occasionally in a tree cavity, cliff crevice or small cave; 1 brood

Eggs/Incubation: 3–7 white eggs; female incubates 30–34 days; male does the most hunting and feeds the nesting female before and after the young hatch

Fledging: 52–56 days; male and female feed young; male does the majority of hunting and brings food to the female, who feeds the chicks; upon leaving the nest (fledging), the young continue to beg for food, at first waiting for the parents to bring food, then following them around to be fed; chicks learn to hunt by watching and copying their parents' behavior, staying with them until the adults prepare for nesting again

Stan's Notes: Well known for nesting in old barns, but also nests in any dark cavity in trees or on cliffs. Readily takes to wooden nest boxes erected by people. Hunts by coursing over open areas after dark, looking and listening for small animals. Employs eyesight mainly, but can hunt in total darkness using hearing alone. Will sway back and forth with head lowered when confronted.

A good friend to farmers. One study showed that over the average 10-year life span of a typical Barn Owl, a single owl will consume approximately 11,000 mice. Based on the amount of food a mouse eats in a day, each year Barn Owls prevent roughly 13 tons of grain and crops from being eaten by mice.

Monogamous and believed to mate for life, with pairs using the same nesting cavity for many years, sometimes for a century or more. Clutch size is dependent on the availability of prey—the more prey, the larger the clutch. The young hatch one per day (asynchronously) over two weeks, creating a range of ages within the nest. Families reside at the same nesting site for generations.

YEAR-ROUND

Barred Owl

Bubo varia

Family: Owls (Strigidae)

Size: L 20–24" (50–61 cm); WS 3–3½' (.9–1.1 m)

Weight: 1½–2 lb. (.7–.9 kg)

Male: Robust brown and gray owl with a large head, gray face, dark brown eyes and horizontal dark barring on the upper chest. Vertical streaks on the lower chest and belly. Yellow bill and feet. No ear tuft "horns."

Female: same as male, slightly larger

Juvenile: light gray with a black face, yellow bill

Habitat: forests, dense woodlands, wooded backyards, near lakes and streams

Food: mice, rabbits, other small to medium animals, small birds, fish, reptiles, amphibians

Sounds: extremely vocal in all seasons and makes many strange sounds; calls 6–8 hoots that sound like "who-who-who-cooks-for-you"; also barks, hisses and gives wheezy, raspy calls repeatedly; female voice is higher than the male; juvenile gives a hissing call when begging for food; day-time calling summons the mate to the nest

Compare: Lacks the "horns" of Great Horned Owl (pg. 225). Eastern Screech-Owl (pg. 201) is less than half the size of the Barred and has ear tufts. Burrowing Owl (pg. 205) is also less than half the size of the Barred and has long legs. Flammulated Owl (pg. 189) is the only other dark-eyed owl, but it is tiny and has short ear tufts.

adult hunting

juvenile

Flight: short broad wings with a wide round tip; slow, deep, full wing beats with much gliding; flies silently

Migration: non-migrator; will move around to find food or establish new territories during winter

Nesting: cavity, large natural hole in a mature tree, cavity must be large enough for an adult and 2–3 young, sometimes uses the same tree cavity for many years; does not add any nesting material, 1 brood

Eggs/Incubation: 2–3 white eggs; female incubates 28–33 days; male does the most hunting and feeds the nesting female before and after the young hatch

Fledging: 42–44 days; female and male feed young; male does the most hunting and brings food to the female, who usually feeds the chicks; males may also sometimes feed chicks before they reach 2 weeks of age; upon leaving the nest (fledging), the young continue to beg for food, chasing parents around after they capture prey; chicks learn to hunt by copying parental behavior; parents feed the young for up to 4 months after they fledge, usually until the end of their first summer; young in a small cavity tend to fledge sooner than those in a large cavity

Stan's Notes: A large owl that can be seen hunting during the day, watching for mice, birds and other prey. Not easily frightened away from its daytime roost. Frequently mobbed by crows. One of the few owls to take fish from a lake or stream. Sits on a branch over the water, watching for fish. Drops down and hovers briefly with several deep wing beats while reaching its feet into the water to snatch a fish.

Prefers dense deciduous woodlands with sparse undergrowth. Might be easy to miss on a tree branch due to the camouflage of its brown-to-gray feathers. Can be attracted with a simple large nest box that has a large opening, attached to a tree. Known to drink and bathe in birdbaths or water puddles.

Entertains people in the area with raucous calls in the evening or during the day. Often sounds like a dog barking just before giving its call of 6–8 hoots. The Great Horned Owl (pg. 225) hoot call differs, sounding like "hoo-hoo-hoo-hoooo."

YEAR-ROUND

Great Horned Owl

Bubo virginianus

Family: Owls (Strigidae)

Size: L 21–25" (53–64 cm); WS 3½–4' (1.1–1.2 m)

Weight: 2½–3¼ lb. (1.1–1.5 kg)

Male: Robust brown-to-gray "horned" owl with bright yellow eyes and a V-shaped white throat that resembles a necklace. Some individuals have tawny orange feathers on the face outlined with a thin black line. Thin horizontal barring on the breast. Stocky round body and a relatively short tail. Large feathered feet.

Female: same as male, slightly larger

Juvenile: similar to adults, gray-to-tan feathers and lacks ear tufts

Habitat: forests, dense woodlands, wooded backyards

Food: mice, rabbits, other small to medium mammals, snakes and insects; routinely takes ducks and other birds

Sounds: very vocal in every season; typical call of 4–6 hoots sounds like "hoo-hoo-hoo-hoooo"; also barks, hisses and repeats wheezy, raspy calls over and over; female voice is higher than that of the male

Compare: Barred Owl (pg. 221) has dark eyes and lacks feather tuft "horns." Larger and more robust than Long-eared Owl (pg. 209), which has a narrower space between its ear tufts. Burrowing Owl (pg. 205) is much smaller, has long legs and lacks ear tufts.

adult landing

juvenile

Flight: long broad wings, cupped or bowed downward during flight; slow, shallow wing beats; silent flight

Migration: non-migrator; moves around in search of food or to establish new territories during winter

Nesting: no nest; takes over the nest of a crow, heron or hawk or uses a partial cavity, stump or broken-off tree; 1 brood

Eggs/Incubation: 2–3 white eggs; female incubates 26–30 days; male does the most hunting and feeds the nesting female before and after the young hatch

Fledging: 30–35 days; male and female feed young; male does the majority of the hunting and brings food to the female, who feeds the chicks; upon leaving the nest (fledging), young still beg for food, chasing parents after they catch prey; chicks learn to hunt by copying their parents' behavior, staying with them until the following winter, when the adults prepare for nesting

Stan's Notes: A resident owl in the South and one of the most common. Often in backyards The first bird to nest each season Starts to mate and lay eggs in late January to March across the South. When the first egg is laid, the female begins incubation and must remain on the nest. The male stands by to sit on the eggs while the female takes a few breaks each day. Aside from this, the female incubates the eggs full-time for nearly a month. Afterward, she sits on her newly hatched chicks (brood) for up to 10 days. Once the chicks get well-developed downy feathers and can control their body temperature, they are left unattended for short periods. Mating starts at 2–3 years. Life span in the wild is 20–25 years.

Can pinpoint prey in total darkness. Able to hear a mouse move under a foot of snow or thick leaf litter. One of the few fearless animals that kills skunks and porcupines. Also called Flying Tiger. Flight feather tips are ragged, resulting in air turbulence reduction and silent flight. Feathery tufts ("horns") on head have nothing to do with hearing; may help to blend its body into the environment. Can lay the tufts flat or hold them up when alert or startled. The neck has 14 vertebrae, enabling the head to swivel up to 280 degrees; the head cannot turn all the way around. Eyelids close from the top down, like those of people.

male

Snowy Owl

Bubo scandiacus

WINTER

Family: Owls (Strigidae)

Size: M 20–24" (50–61 cm); WS 4½–5' (1.4–1.5 m)
F 23–26" (58–66 cm); WS 5–5½' (1.5–1.7 m)

Weight: M 2½–3½ lb. (1.1–1.6 kg); F 4–4½ lb. (1.8–2 kg)

Male: Nearly pure white with a relatively small round head, bright yellow eyes and small dark bill. Varying amounts of small dark markings all over the back and wings. Feet are completely covered with white feathers.

Female: noticeably larger than the male, with many dark bars overall, especially on the top of head, back and wings

Juvenile: similar to the adult female, with dark horizontal bars and a white face; the younger the juvenile, the more barring

Habitat: bogs, meadows, mixed forests, farm fields, airports, frozen lakes or bays during winter, tundra

Food: small and medium-large animals such as mice, lemmings, voles, rabbits and hares, birds

Sounds: normally quiet except during breeding season; gives a high-pitched whistle and growling bark during territorial squabbles or food fights; will repeat a muffled hoot during breeding season

Compare: Our only white owl, rarely confused with any other bird of prey. Slightly larger than Great Horned Owl (pg. 225) which is much darker and has ear tufts.

adult dorsal

juvenile

female

Flight: long broad wings; full, stiff wing beats; silent flight, low to the ground or up to several hundred feet high

Migration: non-migrator to irruptive, moving into northern states; moves into southern states in some years; often found at larger airports

Nesting: ground, often in gravel or atop a hummock; nest is nothing more than a depression that the female scrapes deep enough in the ground to stop eggs from rolling away; 1 brood

Eggs/Incubation: 3–7 white eggs; female incubates 32–34 days; male does the most hunting and feeds the nesting female before and after the young hatch

Fledging: 14–20 days; male and female feed young; male does the majority of hunting and brings food to the female, who feeds the chicks; upon leaving the nest (fledging), the young continue to beg for food, walking around on the tundra while the parents bring food; chicks learn to hunt by watching and copying their parents' behavior, staying with the parents until the first winter

Stan's Notes: The heaviest owl in the world and the second tallest. A nesting bird in the far reaches of Alaska and Canada, known for feeding on lemmings and other small rodents. In most winters, some individuals move; during other winters many move down throughout Canada and northern states in search of food when the supply is not plentiful. Also moves when the local population of owls gets too high. Blends in with snow. Prefers to rest on the ground. Can be active during the day. Unlike many other owls, can be shy and unapproachable.

Has very powerful large feet with extra long talons for hunting rabbits, hares and other larger animals that have the ability to fight back. Does not hide its ground nest since the Snowy is large enough to protect itself and its young successfully most of the time. Clutch size depends on availability of prey. Eggs are the size of chicken eggs. The young hatch several days apart (asynchronously). Families stay together until fall. When young disperse, some fly over 5,000 miles (8,050 km) to establish their own territory. Monogamous and thought to mate for life.

HELPFUL RESOURCES

Cornell Lab of Ornithology Handbook of Bird Biology, Second Edition. Edited by Sandy Podulka, Ronald W. Rohrbaugh Jr. and Rick Bonney. Princeton, NJ: Princeton University Press, 2004.

Field Guide to Hawks of North America, Second Edition, A. Clark, William S. and Brian K. Wheeler. Boston, MA: Houghton Mifflin, 2001.

Hawks in Flight: The Flight Identification of North American Migrant Raptors. Dunne, Peter, David Allen Sibley and Clay Sutton. Boston, MA: Houghton Mifflin, 1989.

Manual of Ornithology: Avian Structure and Function. Proctor, Noble S. and Patrick J. Lynch. New Haven, CT: Yale University Press, 1998.

North American Owls: Biology and Natural History, Second Edition. Johnsgard, Paul A. Washington, DC: Smithsonian Institution, 2002.

Ornithology, Third Edition. Gill, Frank B. New York, NY: W. H. Freeman and Company, 2006.

Owls of the United States and Canada: A Complete Guide to Their Biology and Behavior. Lynch, Wayne. Baltimore, MD: The Johns Hopkins University Press, 2007.

Owls of the World: Their Lives, Behavior and Survival. Duncan, Dr. James R. Toronto, ON: Firefly Books, 2003.

Photographic Guide to North American Raptors, A. Wheeler, Brian K. and William S. Clark. New York, NY: Academic Press, 1999.

Raptors: North American Birds of Prey. Snyder, Noel F. R. and Helen Snyder. Stillwater, MN: Voyageur Press, 1997.

Raptors of Eastern North America: The Wheeler Guides. Wheeler, Brian K. Princeton, NJ: Princeton University Press, 2003.

Raptors of Western North America: The Wheeler Guides. Wheeler, Brian K. Princeton, NJ: Princeton University Press, 2003.

Sibley Guide to Birds, The. Sibley, David Allen. New York, NY: Alfred A. Knopf, 2000.

Emergency

Injured raptors should be turned over to a licensed wildlife rehabilitator. Check local listings for a rehabilitator near you.

Web Pages

The internet is a valuable place to learn more about raptors. You may find studying raptors on the net a fun way to discover additional information about them or to spend a long winter night. These websites will assist you in your pursuit of raptors. If a web address doesn't work (they often change a bit), just enter the name of the group into a search engine to track down the new web address.

Site	Address
Raptor Education Group, Inc.	www.raptoreducationgroup.org
National Eagle Center	www.nationaleaglecenter.org
Wildlife Science Center	www.wildlifesciencecenter.org
American Birding Association	www.americanbirding.org
Cornell Lab of Ornithology	www.birds.cornell.edu
Author Stan Tekiela's home page	www.naturesmart.com

CHECKLIST/INDEX

Use the boxes to check the raptors you've seen.

PHOTO CREDITS

All photos are copyright of their respective photographers.

Deborah Allen: 170 (juvenile perching)

Doug Backlund: 206 (juveniles at burrow), 210 (juvenile)

Paul Bannick/Paul Bannick.com: 190 (juvenile gray)

Giff Beaton: 88

Rick and Nora Bowers: 62 (adult dorsal), 154 (adult Eastern flight), 174 (juvenile flight), 182 (adult flight), 186 (adults perching), 188, 190 (main), 198 (adult gray)

Michael Brown: 78 (adult dorsal)

Richard Cannings: 190 (adult gray perching)

Andy Deegan: 100

Dave Furseth: 80

Reinhard Geisler: 102 (main)

Ned Harris: 134 (juvenile flight)

Marshall J. Iliff: 194 (adult flight)

Phil Jeffrey: 102 (juvenile light flight)

Chris Jimenez: 90 (female flight), 102 (adult dark flight)

Kevin T. Karlson: 54 (top male flight)

Tim Krynak: 90 (juvenile perching)

Greg Lasley Nature Photography: 146 (main)

Tony Leukering: 114 (adult dark)

Bob MacLeod: 130 (main)

Maslowski Wildlife Productions: 202 (adult gray)

Rolf Nussbaumer: 186 (adult flight)

Jake Paredes: 94 (juvenile perching)

Mary Kay Rubey: 124, 126 (juvenile perching)

Stephen J. Shaluta Jr./Dembinsky Photo Associates: 216

Brian E. Small: 90 (main), 128, 134 (juvenile perching), 206 (juvenile Western), 210 (main)

Terry Sohl: 206 (adult Western)

Dick Stilwell: 94 (adult perching)

PHOTO CREDITS *(continued)*

Ted Swem: 194 (juvenile), 230 (juvenile)

Stan Tekiela: 14 (both), 15 (both), 52, 54 (main), 58 (main, adult Taiga flight, both adult Prairie perching), 60, 62 (main), 64, 66 (main, male, adult dorsal), 68, 70 (all except juvenile flight), 72, 74 (main, both adult flight), 76, 78 (all except adult dorsal), 82 (top adult flight), 84, 86 (all), 94 (main), 98 (all insets), 104, 106 (all insets), 108, 110 (main, top adult flight), 112, 114 (main, top adult flight, both juvenile insets), 118 (main, adult Eastern flight, both Florida perching, mother and chicks), 120, 122 (male flight, female flight), 126 (all except juvenile perching), 130 (juvenile), 132, 134 (main), 136, 138 (all), 140, 142 (main, adult male light, all juvenile insets), 144, 146 (adult flight), 148, 150 (all except adult dorsal), 152, 154 (main, adult Harlan's, adult Krider's perching, all juvenile insets), 156, 158 (main, all adult flight), 160, 162 (main, all adult flight), 164, 166 (all), 168, 170 (main, adult fishing), 172, 176, 178 (both insets), 180, 182 (main, chicks), 184, 186 (main), 192, 194 (main), 196, 198 (main), 200, 202 (main, juvenile gray), 204, 206 (main), 208, 210 (all insets except juvenile), 212, 214 (main, adult at nest), 218 (all), 220, 222 (main, juvenile), 224, 226 (all), 228, 230 (main)

Chris Warren: 198 (juvenile gray)

Brian K. Wheeler: 54 (male juvenile), 58 (adult Prairie flight, all juvenile insets), 62 (top adult flight, juvenile), 70 (juvenile flight), 74 (juvenile), 82 (juvenile), 90 (male flight, juvenile flight), 92, 94 (juvenile flight), 102 (adult light, both juvenile dark, juvenile light perching), 114 (adult dorsal), 116, 118 (adult Florida flight), 122 (main, juvenile perching), 130 (adult flight), 142 (both adult dark, adult intermediate), 146 (all juvenile insets), 154 (adult Krider's flight), 158 (both juvenile flight, juvenile light perching, both adult rufous), 162 (both juvenile insets), 170 (juvenile flight), 174 (juvenile perching), 178 (main)

Michael Woodruff: 190 (adult gray flight)

Jim Zipp: 54 (male diving, female flight), 56, 66 (juvenile), 82 (main, adult dorsal), 96, 98 (main), 106 (main), 110 (adult dorsal, all juvenile insets), 118 (both juvenile Eastern), 122 (juvenile flight), 150 (adult dorsal), 158 (juvenile dark perching), 174 (main), 214 (adult flight inset), 222 (adult hunting), 230 (adult dorsal)

To the best of the publisher's knowledge, all photos were of live raptors. Some photos were taken under controlled conditions.

ABOUT THE AUTHOR

Naturalist, wildlife photographer and writer Stan Tekiela is the originator of the popular state-specific field guide series that includes *Birds of Florida Field Guide*. For over two decades, Stan has authored more than 100 field guides, nature appreciation books and wildlife audio CDs for nearly every state in the nation, presenting many species of birds, mammals, reptiles and amphibians, trees, wildflowers and cacti. Holding a Bachelor of Science degree in Natural History from the University of Minnesota and as an active professional naturalist for more than 20 years, Stan studies and photographs wildlife throughout the United States and has received various national and regional awards for his books and photographs. Also a well-known columnist and radio personality, his syndicated column appears in more than 20 newspapers and his wildlife programs are broadcast on a number of Midwest radio stations. He is a member of the North American Nature Photography Association and Canon Professional Services. Stan resides in Victoria, Minnesota, with his wife, Katherine, and daughter, Abigail. He can be contacted via his web page at www.naturesmart.com.